Church Planting--Always in Season
Church Reproduction
Impressions
Pass It On
Seniors in Action
Seniors Serving Seniors
Serving Your 50+ Members
Ten Years Before Sixty-Five
The Third Age in Action

# Marriage Is Fun

## It's Living Together That's Tough

### A. TIMOTHY STARR

iUniverse, Inc.
New York   Bloomington

# Marriage Is Fun
## It's Living Together That's Tough

Scripture quotations are taken from the King James Version of the Bible.

Care has been taken to trace ownership of copyrighted material contained in this book. The published will gladly receive any information that will enable them to rectify any reference or credit line in subsequent editions.

iUniverse books may be ordered through booksellers or by contacting:

iUniverse
1663 Liberty Drive
Bloomington, IN 47403
www.iuniverse.com
1-800-Authors (1-800-288-4677)

ISBN: 978-1-4502-3799-4 (pbk)
ISBN: 978-1-4502-3800-7 (ebk)

Printed in the United States of America

iUniverse rev. date: 8/26/10

# Acknowledgment

This has been a team effort involving many people. I am grateful for their contribution. You will find references and comments from over one hundred singles and couples. In addition, we have comments and contributions from over thirty authors. In each case, every effort has been made to give credit in recognition of using their material.

A special word of thanks to Anne Ford, who has just retired after teaching for more than thirty years. This was her first major project in retirement. She gave considerable time and effort. She corrected spelling, grammar, punctuation, and made the material ready for the editor.

Sara Wood took on the task of being the secretary for the project. Sara is a stay-at-home mom with a great and talented husband and two young children. In her work, she clarified phrasing and improved paragraph flow. She carried this out with great patience.

And so to all who took part in this project, a hearty thank you.

Timothy Starr
July 1, 2010

# Table of Contents

# Foreword

## Why a Book on Remarriage?

There is an increasing number of remarriages, due to the increasing number of divorces. The majority of divorced people will remarry, many within weeks of the divorce. This simply means that as the divorce rate increases, so does the remarriage rate. There is a 45 percent divorce rate for first marriages, but a 65 percent rate for remarriages. Hence, this book offers some help for those taking on marriage the second time around.

There is no doubt that as you enter into marriage again, you are expecting it to be better than your first experience, as well as to be permanent. Of course, this just does not happen without planning and making decisions relative to finances, housing, relatives, and all the other people and things that will come up after the wedding. It is probably true that some folks spend more time considering a new car purchase than planning for remarriage.

The layout of this book is designed specifically to guide you through an examination of your marriage. In the opening chapter, you will read about some of the things that will help your marriage. The second chapter deals with the opposite: things that may hurt a marriage. The next chapter gives insight as to what a good marriage partner is like, followed by twenty testimonies of couples with solid marriages.

An ex-spouse who is unforgiving and bitter can make it hard when a spouse remarries. One chapter is devoted to handling such a spouse. For many couples living through a difficult marriage, divorce is not necessarily the answer. Help and encouragement are offered here.

One chapter is based on Psalm ninety, where Moses, around the age of eighty, gives a six-fold prescription of how life can be significant. In the last chapter, you will find a number of questions people ask as they enter remarriage, along with some answers.

You will find case studies of many people. Yes, their names have been changed, but not the reality of their case.

This book provides practical information. It is sent forth with the understanding that it is not seeking to be a substitute for medical, psychological, or other professional services. If expert counseling is needed, the services of a professional should be sought.

If this book can help you in preparing for a remarriage, then its purpose has been realized.

Wishing you all the best,

Timothy Starr
July 1, 2010

# Introduction

## The Joys and Pitfalls of Remarriage

The vast majority of widowers and divorced people over forty will remarry. Some will do it in haste, plunging into marriage like a cross channel swimmer, who might well develop cramps before he gets out a mile. One missionary, who had been married for nearly thirty years, remarried within three months of burying his wife. Often there is limited thought put into planning and discussing important issues that will affect the new relationship.

> **Marriage is the only game in town where both players can win or lose.**
>
> **—Norman Wright**

William White, a formerly married man, reminds us that:

> Many formerly married are people in transition, wandering for the most part in a no-man's land without a map of the territory, searching for support, guidelines and wisdom.

Others will create fantasy, forgetting the reality they have lived. Now, for many, the divorce rate is not merely from one spouse. I was speaking to a Christian lady who attended the singles group in a large evangelical church. She indicated that she had experienced divorce in her life. Later, I discovered that she had been divorced three times. Another leader told me that he had been divorced three times. I have counseled many who have been divorced two and three times.

This leads us to the conclusion that a remarriage demands as much time and attention as a first marriage. Perhaps more, in fact, due to what has to be unlearned!

> **Remarriage demands as much time and attention as a first marriage.**
> **—Unknown**

Pastors and counselors need to encourage those planning on remarriage to look at finances, housing, beliefs, sexuality, relatives, ex-relatives, and family ties.

This is a big agenda but needs attention, if, indeed, the remarriage is going to be successful.

The following statement by Stuart Briscoe is important to consider:

> There are many people living heaven on earth and they call it marriage and many people living hell on earth and they call it marriage. You can only rejoice with people who have discovered a partner and have been able to work out a relationship under divine principles and with divine enabling that is something close to heaven on earth. And you can also bleed for those people who for a variety of reasons are in a situation where they are living in a daily constant hell.

This book seeks to reaffirm marriage. Marriage can be fun and also good for the health and welfare of people. We know that married people are healthier and for the most part live longer. It is no surprise that married people have more satisfying intimate relationships. Another positive factor for married people is that they have more economic success.

Many often bring into the remarriage experiences and habits from the first marriage. Whether one loses a spouse by death or divorce, a remarriage is a new beginning and the past should be the past. This, however, is easier to say than to experience. Love and being of the same faith are not enough to make for a successful marriage.

In Psychology 101, you studied Abraham Maslow's pyramid of needs. It is good for married people to take his thought to heart. An individual seeks to fulfill his physiological needs, such as food, water, and rest. Next, a person seeks to fulfill safety needs, such as protection from harm. After having the first two needs met, the individual is in need of love and a sense of belonging. Next comes self-esteem, involving receiving recognition as a worthwhile person. Finally, self-actualization completes the pyramid. This is where you desire to live--up to your potential. Now in marriage, the first two are carried out. In remarriage, you need to seek to meet the needs of your spouse for love, belonging, for self-esteem and self-actualization.

**Remarriage is a new beginning and the past should be the past.**

**—Unknown**

Margi Galloway in her counseling manual gives nine suggestions for those planning to remarry:

1. Accept your mate unconditionally.
2. Put the past in perspective.
3. Plant positive words.
4. Encourage in difficult times by building one another up.
5. Give the freedom to fail.
6. Please your mate.
7. Do what is right.
8. Help your mate develop friends.
9. Keep life manageable.

Dr. Neil Warren in his book *Two Dates or Less* suggests each person have a Must Have and Can't Stand List. Draw up a list of twenty-five things one would desire in a mate and the same number one cannot stand in a mate. Reduce each list to ten, listing ten things one wants to have in a mate and ten things one does not want to have in a mate. This quickly will eliminate a number of formerly potential candidates for marriage.

**Marriage is fun, it's living together that's tough.**
**—Ann Landers**

H. Norman Wright, in *Relationships That Work,* gives several factors that would indicate a marriage is off-balance:

1. One person initiates most of the contact in the relationship.
2. One initiates most of the affectionate advances, such as holding hands and kissing.
3. One makes the plan, whereas the other just goes along with it.
4. One sacrifices to do things for the other or makes life more agreeable, without it being reciprocated.
5. One is excited about the relationship while the other person just goes along for the ride.
6. One talks about their relationship and possible future plans, but this strikes an unresponsive chord with the other.

Deciding what one wants in a mate will handle the problem of infatuation, which is sometimes taken for love. Infatuation has to do with outward appearance and feelings. Love has to do with commitment and accepting one's mate without trying to reform them. This is why it is important to choose a mate with similar interests and the same outlook on life.

Imagine a young professional who liked the social life, but his wife had been raised in a quiet home where her parents seldom went out to visit or have friends in. He liked the way she looked. She was pretty, with long hair and lovely features. She liked him because he was tall, handsome, and a professional. It was a case of infatuation. Their commitment lacked love and a deep spirit of oneness.

Another important area in marriage is dealing with conflict. Here one must choose between what is trivial and what is serious. In conflict it is possible to win the battle and lose the war! It is important that one recognizes that we do not need always to have our own way.

> **Be patient and calm—for no one can catch fish in anger.**
>
> **—Herbert Hoover**

The question has been asked: *How can you avoid conflict in marriage?* You cannot avoid conflict in marriage. It is easy to have a clash or a disagreement, especially if one is tired or frustrated. We are human and therefore imperfect. We have feelings. Even our disposition can cause conflict if we are moody or too critical.

The problem is not our differences but our reaction to them. This is where flexibility and tolerance come in, influencing how we relate to conflict. Actually, it can be a positive opportunity for growth, and, if handled in the right way, it can lead to a better and more satisfying relationship.

> **All men are born free and equal—free at least in their right to be different. Some people want to homogenize society everywhere. I am against the homogenizers in art, in politics, in every walk of life. I want the cream to rise.**
>
> **—Robert Frost**

Listening is one of the keys to handling conflict. Do we really understand the problem? Are there parts where we can agree and other parts where we can agree to disagree?

Rob Eager in his book, *The Power of Passion,* discusses the research carried out by Dr. Henry Cloud and Dr. John Townsend. These researchers discovered that unhappy couples usually have the following complaints about their mates:

1. He doesn't listen to me
2. She is so perfect that she can't understand my struggles
3. He seems so distant that I feel alone
4. She always tries to control me
5. He makes promises, but really doesn't follow through
6. He is condemning and judgmental
7. She is always angry at me for something I did or didn't do
8. I tend to be my worst self with her
9. I cannot trust him

Another important consideration for remarriage is the place of sexuality. It is strongly recommended that you practice total abstinence before marriage.

One couple had set the date for their remarriage, and in the midst of planning they came one day to ask if they could change the service from a marriage to a confirmation of their marriage. They felt so sexually attracted toward each other that they went to the courthouse and had a private wedding. However, they wanted a public church service where they could invite their family members and friends. I commended them and we planned a service of reaffirmation of their wedding vows. The Bible does speak to the subject of abstinence in Romans chapter nine.

**My sexuality belongs to God until I marry.**
**—C.S. Lewis**

Richard Cohen speaks about what God meant sex to be:

> Many people have a shortsighted, painfully inadequate understanding of all that God meant sex to be. Sex involves all that you are as a person brought together with another whole person to reflect the complete oneness of Christ and His bride, the church. Sex is special precisely because it's shared with only one person. One author, as he surveyed the wounded, broken lives that flow from an attitude of sexual permissiveness, wisely said, "I have some theories and one of them is that one of the ways you measure love is not with words, but with actions, with commitment, with what you are willing to give up, with what you are willing to share with no one else."

**It is strongly recommended that you practice total abstinence before marriage.**
**—A. Timothy Starr**

Married people need to remember the difference between sexuality and affection. When the late Ann Landers polled her readers on their thoughts and feelings about sex, she found that 72 percent of the women said that they would be content to be held lovingly rather than actually having sex. The point of the matter is that the wife looks upon sex from a relational viewpoint and the man completely separated from the relational aspect. Those ready to experience a remarriage would do well to remember the five-fold ways of manifesting love that Gary Chapman and others have written about:

1. Gift Giving
2. Words of Encouragement
3. Sharing Time
4. Touching
5. Serving

It has been said again and again that words can have an important role in married life. According to Cliff Barrows of the Billy Graham Evangelistic Team, there should be in our vocabulary the following:

> I was wrong.
> I am sorry.
> Please forgive me.
> I love you.

One area of concern for those previously married is whether or not you are comparing the one you are about to marry with your ex. Let's face it, it is impossible not to compare, whether it be favorably or unfavorably. One widow in her early seventies married the widower of her best friend. As we discussed an area of tension, she admitted that it is impossible not to do some comparison. The important factor is not to let this influence your future relationship with the one you are now marrying.

**The soul would have no rainbow had the eyes no tears.**
**—John V. Cheney**

It is advisable not to rush into marriage. Initial loneliness and sorrow leave people too vulnerable to make sound choices. Dr. Ed Pakes, a Toronto psychiatrist who leads courses on grief and mourning, says:

> Good mourning requires devoting time to deal with our
> grief reaction and thinking through the whole experience
> of what was that person's relationship to you.

From time to time we have had to deal with the issue of a summer and winter marriage. For example, here's an eighty-five year old gentleman planning to marry a lady in her late fifties. Of course, you have the usual criticism that he is robbing the cradle or she is marrying him for his money. It is wise to point out that there are serious adjustments to be considered. There are experiences he has been through, due to his age, that she still has ahead of her. When he is ninety, she will be sixty. Will she be ready to slow down to his pace?

**Another factor to consider in remarriage has to do**
**with children from the first or other marriage.**
**—Unknown**

You may think this doesn't apply to you if your children are grown. Yes, perhaps the children are on their own and have long since left the home. Have they? Consider how many return due to a failed marriage or financial problems. It would appear that children always will be part of the remarriage, in one way or another. We must ask the parties if they are ready for this continuous interruption.

Now there are other issues that need to be thought through carefully. Do you really enjoy your spouse's grown children? How would you handle the situation if one grown son or daughter had to come home for a period of time? Would you be prepared to loan the son or daughter money if the need arose? You can think of other situations that could be raised.

There should be times when a parent spends time with his or her biological grown children, either as a group or as an individual. The other spouse needs to encourage this and not feel resentful.

You have lost your spouse, either by death or divorce. Now what? Yes, you are lonely. You desire companionship. You found someone like yourself.

**The heart is slow to learn what the swift mind beholds at every turn.**

**—Edna St. Vincent Millay**

Now what? The following questions appeared in *Primetime,* which is published by the Senior Ministries of the Assembly of God. It is suggested you take time to consider these questions.

Family Concerns

1. Do your families know each other? If so, are they compatible?
2. Do the adult children of both parties approve of the possibility of marriage?
3. If there are children still living at home, do they accept you?
4. If there are negative responses, are you willing to wait until they are resolved?
5. Can you willingly accept each other's children just as they are?

6. Does your friend have the freedom to make his or her own decisions?
7. Is your friend in relatively good health? If not, can you accept the limitations?

Financial Concerns

1. Do you need a prenuptial agreement?
2. Can your finances be set up in trust funds that will protect both families?
3. Will you have an adequate income to live comfortably?
4. What kind of debt does each of you owe?
5. Will you have a joint bank account or separate accounts? If separate accounts, decide ahead of time who is responsible for which financial obligations.
6. Are most of your financial philosophies compatible?
7. Do you have up-to-date wills?

Housing Concerns

1. Do each of you own property? If so, where will you live?
2. Would you both consider selling your property and buying something together?
3. How will you blend two households of furniture?
4. Will marriage force one person to move to another city?
5. If you choose to live in a house already owned by one of you, can you live with the memories of the first spouse without letting them interfere with your relationship with the new spouse?
6. Are you willing to share extra household items with the children rather than sell everything you do not need? There may be things of sentimental value to family members that need to be passed on to the next generation.
7. If necessary, are you willing to live in an apartment complex rather than buy or build another house?
8. Discuss and come to a conclusion regarding where you will live after marriage.

Now it is time to get into the various ways to make any marriage, whether it be the first, the second, or even the third, successful and delightful.

# CHAPTER ONE

## Why Some Remarriages Succeed

This one chapter alone can help prepare those planning to remarry. It also can serve as an inventory for married people. It is never too late to improve a marriage, and this can serve as a guide.

# 1—Commitment

## Tea in Bed

---

The memorial service for Bert Smith was held in a Baptist chapel on a cool Monday evening. There was no casket, as his remains had been cremated the preceding week. In the chancel area, the family had brought in the various things that Bert had used both at work and in recreation: gardening equipment, a kayak, cameras, an engineering book, and maps.

After the opening hymn and comments by the pastor, the service was turned over to family members. All five children went up and took an item and related it to their father, giving a loving tribute. However, before they took their turns, Bert's wife, Sharon, stood and walked up to the chancel and picked up a cup and saucer. We all wondered what was next. Let's hear it in her own words:

> I suppose you are wondering what I am doing with this cup and saucer. Well, when my husband Bert proposed to me, I told him that if he wanted me to marry him, then he would have to bring me a cup of tea in bed before I got up! And do you know, for forty years he did that, except for the days when he was out of town.

Now, this is what you call committed! Reliable! Steadfast! Dependable! This was their time to share their schedule and talk over concerns for their own relationship and family ties. This gave them time to strengthen their faith and to pray together.

**It is simplicity of intention that gives consistency to life.**

**—William C. Braithwaite**

A cup of tea kept them together? No! No! No! That cup of tea was only a symbol of their relationship with each other and the activities related to it. Here was a husband who was committed to his wife. He kept his word. She could trust him with her life and her family. What more could any wife desire?

## 2—Accountability

## To God and Your Spouse

In a Christian marriage, God has an important part. The marriage ceremony includes the phrase, "Do you, in the presence of God?" The marriage vow is between you and your spouse and your God. Long before creation, God had in mind the union of one man and one woman in marriage.

This is such an important truth that God illustrates it in the love that Christ has for the church, as explained in Ephesians chapter five. It is rendered in verse thirty-two: "This is a great mystery: but I speak concerning Christ and the church." What is the mystery?

Marriage is to be an illustration of the union between Christ and His church. Christ is the bridegroom, the church is His bride. Thus, the husband is to give an account of his relationship and love for his wife to God our Creator. Husbands are accountable to God! This is a unique reality.

**Moreover it is required in stewards, that a man be found faithful.**
**—1 Corinthians 4:2**

Marriage takes on really serious proportions when the husband realizes that treating his wife with respect and support is a high Christian responsibility. You can imagine how the wife will respond to such a godly husband. Now, where does the wife fit into the picture? Well, kindness begets kindness. The delightful ministry of the husband generally brings the same response from a wife. A fine biblical illustration of a husband obeying God is seen in the life of Hosea and his marriage to Gomer. Although she committed one sinful act after another, Hosea kept his marital vows. He recognized his accountability to God.

**Be the living expression of God's kindness, in your face, your eyes, your smile, your greeting.**
**—Mother Teresa**

Jack Gibson was a tower of strength in his church. At his job at the foundry, he was responsible for over a thousand men. Yet his wife, who did not profess faith, was a thorn in his flesh. Although Jack tried many times to keep his marriage intact, his wife finally removed herself; and for all intents and purposes, the marriage was over. Sometimes the road to marital bliss can be hard, as was the case in Jack Gibson's marriage. However, in the marriage of Robertson and Muriel McQuilkin, we see a different type of commitment resulting from a very different struggle.

Dr. McQuilkin was the very capable president of Columbia Bible College for many years. When Muriel, his wife, came down with Alzheimer's disease, he resigned his post as president. His board sought to persuade him to stay on. They offered to get help for his wife and to assist him with her needs, in an effort to keep him as their leader.

This was his response:

> No, thank you for your consideration, but over forty years ago I made a commitment to Muriel, in the presence of God, that I would care for her in sickness and in health. Now I must keep my vow. I made a promise, and with the help of God, I intend to keep it. I'm a person of my word. I'm in this for life.

And so he carried out his resignation and devoted his whole time to the care and support of his wife.

## One Small Flower a Week

Jack Flestra was born into a poverty-stricken family. His parents were missionaries in South America. There were eight children in the family, and it was difficult to find enough shelter, clothing, and food to go around. Yet, in one way after another, the family's material needs were met as Jack's parents pressed forward in their ministry.

Coming home to where his grandparents lived, Jack met and married Deedee, who came from a background similar to his own. The two had very little, but were content to be married and to be in the ministry. Mind you, it was tough going to seminary when they had few resources and a newborn child. However, both Jack and Deedee had very little as children growing up, and it was not too challenging for them to handle poverty in their own marriage.

**The most important thing in any relationship is not what you get back but what you give.**
**—Eleanor Roosevelt**

Upon seminary graduation, the Flestras were called to serve a small church in northern Ontario. The town of Cochrane had a population of four thousand, divided equally between native people and Caucasians. Although the remuneration was limited, the church did provide a fine parsonage. In this situation, Jack gave thought as to how he might show his love for his wife in a tangible way. He arranged with the florist in town to pick up one single flower each Friday. This was his way of showing his wife how much she meant to him. Actually, the florist was so impressed with Jack's desire to honor his wife that she arranged to have a choice flower for him, each Friday, and at an affordable price.

Deedee came to appreciate this weekly gift. She was never sure of what it would be, but she knew it was an expression of love and fidelity. Yes, she opened her heart and soul to Jack and their marriage blossomed. The florist could not keep from telling others about this act of love. Before long, all the townspeople knew about this weekly gift from the man of the cloth to his wife.

Although the church had a small congregation, it also gained the attention of the town, as a result of the minister's actions. When a minister makes such an impression in a small community, it does not take long before a larger church extends an invitation for him to come and be their pastor. With deep emotion, Jack and Deedee bade farewell to the small church in Cochrane. It was not so much what or how Jack had preached, but that he lived out his sermons before the people. Jack had put feet to his messages, and everyone was blessed by his practical demonstration of love for his wife.

## Dressing/Cleaning /Lifting/Shopping

Joni Tada was a natural athlete, who enjoyed outdoor sports like running, skating, and swimming. At eighteen, she was coming into full strength until she jumped into the waters of Chesapeake Bay and hit the bottom with a severe jolt. It left her paralyzed from the neck down. Her whole life was changed in a second. Unable to use her feet and hands in a normal way, she was now confined to a wheelchair for the rest of her life.

**You don't let anyone suffer alone.**

**—Unknown**

This would leave most young people in a spirit of deep and hopeless depression. Many would assume her aspiration of marriage was swept away, for who would want to marry a paralyzed person? Gainful employment? And recreation? And travel? All gone! Not so with Joni. She sensed that God had a plan for her life, including a marvelous husband, in the person of Ken Tada. Ken was a physical trainer with strong muscles and a tender heart. He took it upon himself to care for Joni for the rest of her life and married her with this in mind. This meant that he would have to be with Joni twenty-four hours a day! In short, he would be living her life. He dressed her, bathed her, cleaned the house, and shopped for her. Everything! Ken and Joni have made it through the difficult struggles that have come their way. They have demonstrated how you can have a marriage that lasts a lifetime.

## Know How to Handle Anger

When two imperfect people marry, there will be disagreements and problems. Couples must work out how they are going to handle conflict when it arises. Many couples revert to the methods their parents used. One parent may have exploded while the other remained calm and quiet. The real problem comes when the wife and husband become angry with each other at the same time. One rule that some couples employ is an understanding that when one uses a phrase such as, "That's enough," or "Let's carry on tomorrow," the conflict stops immediately.

It is wise not to avoid conflict, but to face it with a determination to clear the air. Gary Smalley says conflict is like starting a fire. You have to learn to handle it properly or it can tear you and your spouse apart. So the real problem is not the anger or conflict, but how you deal with it.

**All married couples should learn the art of battle as they should learn the art of love. Good battle is objective and honest—never vicious or cruel. Good battle is healthy and constructive, and brings to a marriage the principle of equal partnership.**
**—Ann Landers**

Glen and Gail Anderson were eighty-one and seventy-two when they married. Both their spouses had passed away. The two couples were part of the same church and knew each other well. Both could get hot under the collar at the drop of a hat. Gail, knowing Glen so well, would back off and hold her anger for another day. She was able to confront Glen in her own time and in her own way. And they were both able to express their needs effectively. In this way, they maintained their own self-esteem and their marriage.

As they shared their lives, Glen and Gail had to rethink how they handled anger. They did not want to repeat mistakes made in their first marriages. However, they each were different from their spouse's first husband or wife. It took time for the two to adjust to each other and develop a fine relationship. They recognized that they both could not win, but that compromise was the best way to handle the situation.

In dealing with conflict, it is important that each partner listens and understands what the anger is about. It is best to hear your spouse out. Ask questions to get to the root of the matter.

## 6—Carelessness

### Forgetting Special Days

---

There are three special days in the life of a wife that her husband should never forget: her birthday, their anniversary, and Valentine's Day! This was a lesson that Gary Smalley learned by experience. This is what he said:

> Before our first Valentine's Day celebration, Norma had never cooked a roast beef dinner. She had turned our small dining room into a romantic harbor with a new tablecloth, candles, cardboard hearts, the works. Most men would have been alert to the fact that it was Valentine's Day from billboards, commercials, and card displays in the stores. Not me. I had no idea. I had prepared nothing. I phoned home that day around two in the afternoon. "Hey, Hon," I said. "I have a basketball game tonight at the college. I'm playing at six o'clock. Will you come and watch?" There was dead silence on the other end of the phone.
>
> "Do you know what day this is?"
>
> "Uh . . . no."
>
> "It's Valentine's Day, and I've cooked you a special dinner," she said. "I've been working on it all day."
>
> I knew I was in trouble, but I couldn't miss the game. I yelled out my first reaction without thinking, much less listening, protecting my desires and my agenda. I made a dishonoring statement that continues to haunt me thirty-five years later . "I promised the guys I would be there, and they don't have enough players without me," I said. And that night when I got home from the game I was excited and called out to Norma: "Hey, honey, guess what," I shouted, bounding into the kitchen. "We won! Isn't that great?" No response from Norma. Then I saw the cold roast beef and the melted candles and the now forlorn-looking cardboard hearts.

Gary goes on to describe how much he failed his wife that first Valentine's Day. But it was a lesson he learned for life.

**Selective memory is the art of forgetting our failures while remembering the lessons learned.**
**—Richard Exley**

Carelessness can be seen in forgetting special days and activities, overlooking responsibilities, and leaving undone things that ought to be done.

## 7—Acceptance

### He Did Not Take His Wife for Granted

---

It was at a New Year's Eve party that ninety-three-year old Jim Little was interviewed. Five years earlier, his wife of sixty-five years had died of cancer. Jim had been a senior executive with a large municipal hydro corporation. In his work, he was called upon to put in long hours of work, regardless of holidays, working with people of all ages and personalities. Yet, in all his years and busy life, he never neglected his wife. He never took her for granted, but really treated her like a queen. She was the woman of his dreams and the love of his life.

**Proving what is acceptable unto the Lord.**
**—Ephesians 5:10**

When he knew his position would occupy him for the evening, Jim would call and let his wife know. In his relationship with her, he was thoughtful and considerate. From time to time, after a fine meal, he would write a short note of thanks to his wife. Jim would take time to talk with his wife, recognizing that, as a stay-at-home mom, she did not have the opportunities to socialize or to share ideas and concepts with others.

Together, Jim and his wife raised a family of three. As the children grew, they were brought into the evening fellowship and conversations. Jim recognized that his wife was special and treated her as such. It is no surprise to hear that his children turned out well and that two of his grandchildren are working toward doctorate degrees. The other is in high school and might follow suit.

## 8—Compatibility

### Agreement—Oneness

A basic principle of life for positive relationships is compatibility. This is also a biblical principle. Amos 3:3 says: "Can two walk together, except they be agreed?" Compatibility starts when two people find they enjoy doing the same thing, whether it be music, drama, sports, or theatre. It is helpful to have common ground when it comes to friends, finances, and social interests.

> **What counts in making a happy marriage is not so much how compatible you are, but how you deal with incompatibility.**
>
> **—George Levinger**

Rev. Frank Pickering and his wife, Marion, recently celebrated their sixty-first wedding anniversary and looked back on their lives together. They both became Christians when they were small children. When they met each other, it was love at first sight. The two have graduate degrees and are ardent readers. Languages come naturally to them: English, French, Japanese, Greek, and Hebrew. Even in their dress, they have the same approach. They do not go for loud apparel, but quiet tones.

In their conservations, Frank and Marion are deliberate and cautious. The two display a mild disposition. You soon sense their warmth for each other and how they minister to one another. One can understand how the Pickerings were able to spend forty years in a Japanese city as missionaries. They saw limited results, but they had the patience and the fortitude to stay and to serve the Lord there faithfully. Their marriage played a major part in their lives. In essence, compatibility in spiritual beliefs, energy level, intelligence, interests, activities, and values is important. It is not necessary to have identical personalities, as differences can complement each other. It is more important to have a mate who has similar core values. Is there common ground in friends, finances, and social interests between you and your mate?

## 9—Matchmaker

### Did God Bring You Together?

The business of real estate has never been an easy one. However, in times like today, the pressures are mighty and the time required for achieving goals is great. Despite being busy in their work, the Chuas have taken time to nurture their love for one another and to build a successful marriage.

> **Reflect upon your present blessings, of which every man has many—not on your past misfortunes, of which all men have some.**
>
> **—Charles Dickens**

Laura and Andy Chua are prominent realtors in the Asian community. As a matter of fact, at the time of this writing, they are actively involved in building a twenty-five million dollar complex for seniors. Although they are very busy people, their closeness to each other is very evident. Their strong marital bond can be traced back to the place that God has had in their lives. The Chuas acknowledge that Jesus Christ is their Matchmaker. This is the way they describe their relationship:

> Jesus Christ is the foundation of our marriage. The love, respect, and trust that we have for each other have bonded us together through Jesus Christ. He has given us the strength to stay together. It would appear that couples who recognize that God brought them together sense a greater responsibility to make their marriage work. They are able to overlook petty things and to accept each other.

## 10—Celebration

### Let's Have a Party!

It is interesting to note how celebrating special days can create a deep bond between husband and wife. However, there are a lot of days in the year. After New Year's Day, you have Martin Luther King Day in January or the Family Day in Ontario, and either in March or April you have the Easter weekend. On into May, you have Victoria Day in Canada and Memorial Day in the United States, followed by the summer holidays. In September is Labor Day, and on the second Monday in October there is Thanksgiving in Canada, and on the fourth Thursday of November you have Thanksgiving in the United States . . . all leading up to Christmas. Of course you have birthdays, baptisms, and other family celebrations. There are other activities of a special nature that call for a celebration, such as the annual football title in February. There may be the quarterly social in your home for your Sunday school class.

**Laughter is a great tranquilizer with no side effects.**
**—Arnold Glasow**

Miriam, a special education schoolteacher, and her husband, Glenn Johnson, make much of special days. Together, they open their spacious home and celebrate with family and friends. Working together makes it a family project and assists in keeping up their close relationship.

John Rehm in his book, *Toward Commitment,* discusses celebrations:

I learned from Diane the great value of having the four of us celebrate the events of the calendar year, including the Christian holidays, together. (40)

## Will That Be Cash or a Credit Card?

Money is an issue that can have a major impact on a marriage. Many couples do not discuss it ahead of time and so must settle things on their honeymoon. Who is going to be the treasurer? How does one spouse go about getting money? How much should each spouse get and how often? Have we set limits on how much we spend for different items? These and many other questions must be settled in the opening weeks of marriage.

> **But my God shall supply all your need according to his riches in glory by Christ Jesus.**
> **—Philippians 4:19**

An agreed-upon budget needs to be established. The budget should include a ten percent savings component and another percentage for charity. It is best to do all this before a family comes along.

> **About the time we think we can make ends meet, someone moves the ends.**
> **—Herbert Hoover**

Don Cameron, a retired Bell Telephone executive, and his wife, Phyllis, were approaching their sixtieth wedding anniversary. In response to my interview, he indicated a number of things that have helped them over the years. This is what he wrote:

> During the first year of our marriage, some fifty-seven years ago, my wife Phyllis and I committed our lives to our Lord Jesus Christ. This act has provided us with strength and guidance throughout our life together. Made us perfect? No! Taught us the meaning and value of humbling ourselves before God and man? Yes! Early in our journey of faith, we began to realize that God seldom does what it is our responsibility to do. For instance, He commands us to, "Trust in the Lord with all your heart and lean not on your own understanding. In all your ways acknowledge Him and He will direct your paths" (Prov. 3:5, 6).

My wife and I have always shown each other a high degree of respect and trust. We never take each other for granted. We have found that good communication in our marriage works well in promoting the respect and trust that we expect from each other. We discovered that a major key to a successful relationship is to be good financial managers. This has involved strong discipline, especially in our materialistic society, where marketing people urge us to spend dollars that we don't always have. In our view, poor management of personal finances can and does fracture relationships.

We realize that it takes a lot of hard work on the part of both spouses for a marriage to be successful. Nothing is for free. But our God has richly blessed us and we praise His name continually.

## 12—Appreciation

## That Was a Fine Meal

A word of appreciation in season is like the fresh morning dew. It lifts up the spirit when you recognize someone near and dear for a job well done. They realize that you have noticed what they have been doing and are likely to respond positively. It is good to praise your spouse even over small things.

**You can attract more bees with honey than with vinegar.**

**—Unknown**

In an American study, it was discovered that women are blessed when they are told that they are loved, appreciated, and valued. Gary Smalley has penned these words:

Catch your partner doing something good and praise the heck out of it.

Jim and Shirley Simpson would "needle" each other several times a day. They would criticize one another for the small aggravations that occurred throughout the day. Perhaps Shirley had overcooked the meat or Jim had left a hammer on the kitchen table after hanging a picture. Henry and Pam from another state came to visit them for several days. Henry was known for complimenting his wife often. Shirley told him one morning that he had complimented his wife more times that morning than Jim had complimented her all year.

**I can live two months on a good compliment.**
**—Mark Twain**

It is true that complimenting is always in season. In Proverbs 31:31, Solomon, who knew much about women, tells how one woman's household praises her:

Give her of the fruit of her hands; and let her own works praise her in the gates.

It is impossible to live with a wife without having opportunities to give her strong feedback for her domestic ministry.

## Fidelity in Word and Deed

It was an emotional experience to hear a pastor say about a departed member in the celebration of his life and ministry:

> Our brother was married to the love of his life for over forty years. He had eyes for only one woman, his wife.

What an amazing remark in this day when so many marriages are breaking up. This type of commitment begins with being committed to God! The word *committed* means "binder" or "pledge." A committed individual demonstrates a lifestyle of fidelity in word and in deed. Actually, it begins in your mind, what you are thinking. This is what Jesus says in Matthew 5:27, 28:

> Ye have heard that it was said by them of old time, Thou shalt not commit adultery: But I say unto you, That whosoever looketh on a woman to lust after her hath committed adultery with her already in his heart.

Few things encourage a wife more than a good and faithful husband. Husbands and wives who honor their promises are people of integrity.

**Every enduring marriage involves an unconditional commitment to an imperfect person—your spouse.**
**—Gary Smalley**

## Keep the Fire Burning

Intimacy should be a lifelong marital experience. A fine definition of intimacy is given by David Stoop in his book *The Intimacy Factor:*

> Intimacy is the joyful union that comes when two people learn together how to give love and how to accept love.

There are many ways to give intimacy besides the exercise of sex. For instance, there is the way we look at our spouse, and the way we reach out to touch our spouse, and even the way we respond to them verbally. Calling on the phone unexpectedly or writing a short love note adds to the passion of intimacy. A surprise gift of candy or a flower is a manifestation of love and affection. A hug or a squeeze can show our closeness. Just sitting together and discussing the issues of the day or planning a vacation together indicates the aspiration of love.

> **The need for emotional intimacy is one of the greatest reasons for the affair.**
>
> **—Norm Wright**

Neil Armstrong was a six-foot-four, athletic man, known for his overt affection to his wife Margaret. When she died of cancer, Neil remarried a divorcee, Lynda, within a few weeks. Lynda had had a difficult divorce and longed for love and affection. She found all she could want in Neil. He would come to a morning committee meeting late, but without embarrassment claimed he had "overslept." We knew what he meant!

## 15—Faith

### Can Two Walk Together Without Agreement?

No, it is not necessary to have oneness in faith, but it sure helps! We are seeing more mixed marriages today, and the trend will continue. For many years, mixed marriages tended to be between Jews, Roman Catholics, or Protestants, but now it is not uncommon to see other world religions as well. Of course, it is not much of a problem if neither one is practicing their faith. However, it is not easy for a married person to practice his faith alone. He sits in the service alone. He has no one to discuss the service with later on in the day. And of course, when the first child comes along, you will want him raised in your own religious tradition.

> **Nothing doth keep men out of the church, and drive men out of the church, as breach of unity.**
> **—Francis Bacon**

In one case, Shelly was raised a Lutheran while Dan a Baptist. They wanted to go to church together and so they chose a different denomination, apart from one either had been raised in. More and more couples are handling it this way. People are finding that a common faith and worship service, along with the friends you meet at church, mean much to the joy of a marriage. It is best to have this settled before marriage, so it does not become an issue later.

## 16—Self-Esteem

## I Am What I Am by the Grace of God!

Having confidence in yourself is important in developing proper relationships with others. Some folks have such a low image of themselves that they have to reach up to touch bottom! Those who are very hard on themselves often can be hard on others, especially those who are close to them.

Many people cannot accept compliments, or they wonder if there is an underlying motive behind them. Others can accept compliments directed to others, but not to themselves.

> **Things don't go wrong and break your heart so you can become bitter and give up. They happen to break you down and build you up so you can be all that you were intended to be.**
> **—Charles "Tremendous" Jones**

Positive self-esteem can help you with your relationships and behavior. It gives you what one might call self-worth. It is important that you recognize your positive traits. What do you like about yourself? Others like those traits about you, too. There is nothing wrong with liking the person you are. After all, this is why your spouse married you.

## 17—In-Laws Can Help a Marriage

## In-Laws Can Hurt a Marriage

When one marries, he or she is not marrying an individual, but into a tribe of people, beginning with and foremost, the immediate in-laws. Wise is the individual who is able to develop a strong genuine bond of love with them. This can be accomplished by extending one's self to the in-laws with love and affection. After all, they made it possible for you to marry your spouse and the least you can do is to be a grateful and loving spouse to their grown child.

With the full approval of your spouse, think of ways you can serve your in-laws. Special occasions such as birthdays and anniversaries are occasions where one can really show affection and love. Make much of religious special days if your in-laws are active in their faith. Include them, again if your spouse agrees, on short trips and other social events.

In-laws usually like to fuss over their grandchildren. Make arrangements for them to do this. Have the grandchildren write and phone their grandparents. This will strengthen the bonding.

Giving your child a first or second name of an in-law can do wonders. In many cases, unless care is taken, that individual child could become a favorite! That is the last thing you want to see.

It is always in season to remind your in-laws what a splendid job they did in raising your spouse. Be specific and name particular characteristics that help to make your marriage such a delight.

In-laws must remember that their married child is first a spouse and then their child, not the other way around. They have left the biological home and are now creating a new one, which must have the priority.

If the in-laws experience separation or divorce, then things become complicated. There are now two sets of parents to please. Compromises must be made on special days of the year such as Thanksgiving and Christmas. Of course, the kids like it as now they get a double set of gifts on birthdays and at Christmas.

In the final analysis, the wife has an important part in helping to develop the right relationship between her mother and her husband. She understands them and knows how to handle them. The wife desires to show her mother how well she can handle her home, including her husband. To some degree there is competition as to who can make the best wife and mother!

In-laws would do well to keep in mind that the wife is a key to their relationship with the grandchildren! In many ways the mother can control the degree of time her children will have with their grandparents.

All this goes to show how much influence in-laws can have in the success of a marriage.

This chapter is useful for re-evaluating personal relationships, before and after marriage. Nothing is like the bond between a husband and a wife. It should be the greatest of all earthly experiences. Our parents cannot make it that. Our friends cannot do it. It must come from our hearts. What can be better than two people, a man and a woman, committed to each other in marriage?

# Think About This!

Of all the various aspects of a successful marriage, discussed in this chapter, which do you think are the three most important?

# CHAPTER TWO

# Why Some Remarriages Fail

### Twenty-Five Reasons Why Some Marriages Fail

With a 45 percent divorce rate for first marriages and 65 percent for second marriages, it is important to understand what leads to the dissolution. Being forewarned can give a couple time to plan in order to handle the various pitfalls. It has been helpful for me to interview a sizeable number of divorced people. Those interviewed represent a cross section of society: doctors, lawyers, teachers, ministers, nurses, and secretaries. Let's look at some of the things that can lead to failure in a marriage and some examples from the experiences of different couples.

Many people have certain illusions about marriage. When they discover that marriage is not what they expected, they experience a huge let-down. One's background and upbringing determine to some extent what they are expecting in marriage. How do we handle expectations? In some cases, they need to be lowered. In other cases, they need to be raised. We need to understand life as it is and choose to live within realistic parameters.

> **Everything that irritates us about others can lead us to an understanding of ourselves.**
>
> **—Carl Jung**

Clint Anstey went to live in a large city just after World War 1. He looked sharp in his uniform. Gladys Emerson had just graduated from a private high school. When they met, it was love at first sight. The courtship period lasted only a few months. They married and settled down to raise a family. Now, Clint was a farm boy raised in a country village. His mother was a superb cook and homemaker. He had five sisters who spoiled him. When he got married, he was expecting a clean house, satisfying meals, and someone to meet his every need. Gladys was raised in England in an upper-class family, where her every need was met immediately. Her mother died when she was a teenager. Within a few months, her dad remarried and moved to America. Gladys's stepmother did not take to her stepdaughter, and so she arranged for her to do her high school education in a private institution some twenty-five hundred miles away.

You can appreciate that Clint's and Gladys's expectations were different and were far from being met. Clint was anticipating a home life where the meals would be tasty, the house clean, and that Gladys would stay at home with the children. Gladys, on the other hand, was looking forward to a business career with money to spend and a husband who would wait on her, hand and foot, and meet her every need. As it turned out, only Clint's expectation of having children was met. He and Gladys had four boys, one dying at childbirth. Gladys was pleased with giving birth to her boys, but otherwise felt unsatisfied with the marriage.

It wasn't long before the two started arguing, which in turn led to outright war! Things as they were could not go on. Finally, Clint found another woman, much to his liking, who would meet his needs. Gladys, several years later, found a husband who would spoil her!

**A great marriage is not when the "perfect couple" comes together. It is when an imperfect couple learns to enjoy their differences.**

**—Dave Meurer**

Now, as you examine their marriage, it is easy to see that it was not built on equality and trust. Clint and Gladys did not discuss their personal viewpoints or share their expectations of marriage. They were set in their ways and were not ready to change. Polly Eisendrath, in her book, *You're Not What I Expected,* gives Dr. Harry Sullivan's definition of *intimacy* as "a special kind of relationship based on reciprocity, trust and equality." (11) This is exactly what Clint and Gladys did not have. Although they were churchgoers, neither one applied their faith in their marriage.

It is amazing how many husbands are not able to leave and cleave (Gen. 2:24). Without this leaving and cleaving, it is impossible for a husband to give himself to his wife fully. Marriage is all about creating a new family unit in life, one that is separate from the one in which you were raised. In our American culture, no house is large enough for both wife and mother.

Bill Hampton, a neurosurgeon, was married to Betty, a high school teacher. Betty discovered that her husband could not separate himself from his mother. This is what she said:

Many factors contributed to the failure of my marriage, but I believe chief among the factors is my former husband's inability to separate from his birth family, especially from his mother. As an only son, his mother and sister doted on him, and no one could ever be good enough for him. In his late fifties, he continues to live with his mother.

In this case, Bill's mother had too much of a hold on his life. He really was not independent, nor able to stand against her strong influence. Though he was a brilliant doctor, Bill was not willing to realize that his wife should now replace his mother.

A beautiful fifty-two-year old banker was dating a fine fifty-eight-year old gentleman. He was all a lady could want for in a husband. She was all a man could want for in a wife. He would come over to her apartment two to three times a week. They usually ended up in hugs and kisses that, at times, grew intense. They did not practice sex, although they were tempted to. Both had strong convictions on pre-marital sex. It was on such occasions that she would bring up the subject of marriage. When she did, he would revert to the fact that he was living with his ninety-one-year old mother. Even though his mother was still able to drive and be quite active, he didn't feel he could move out and leave her on her own.

His mother liked his lady friend, but she did not try to influence her son to marry her. It did not occur to her that, once she passed away, her son could be alone for the rest of his life, whereas now he had an opportunity to marry a most exceptional woman.

**Whenever I date a guy, I think, "Is this the guy I want my children to spend their weekends with?"**
**—Rita Rudner**

A young student pastor started dating a woman who would be an excellent minister's wife. But his mother had a very strong hold on him. When it came time for the wedding, the young man wanted to invite his divorced father, but his mother put up such a fuss that he did not do it. Later on, he admitted that not inviting his father was a major blunder and that he was very sorry for having let his mother control him to such a degree.

Ask any counselor, and they will tell you that this is one of the most difficult situations to handle. In fact, as long as the third party is around, it will be a challenge to have real restoration. You see this alarming factor in our movies and in our newspapers. Infidelity can damage an individual's self-image. The betrayed individual feels rejected and often does not know what went wrong. The unfaithful spouse is displaying a lack of integrity. It is a nightmare when an unsuspecting spouse discovers betrayal, especially if the individual is a friend of the family!

> **The need for emotional intimacy is one of the greatest reasons for the affair.**
>
> **—Norm Wright**

Mary Ann Ferguson and her husband Joe were close friends with Jordan and his wife Judy. They went on holidays together—camping, cruises, and hikes. Joe, a salesman, starting calling his wife to say that he was working late and that she should not wait for him for supper. Actually, he was eating with Judy, whenever her husband Jordan was out of town on business. One day, Mary Ann got a phone call from a friend, who told her that her husband was having dinner with Judy. That night, when Jordan got home, he found Mary Ann in the living room with red eyes. She had been crying. She asked him if what her friend had said was true, to which he replied that it was and told her everything. Neither one slept the whole night as they talked about the situation. She asked him to leave and that was the end of their marriage.

Can you appreciate what it would be like to lose your spouse to one of your best friends? Mary Ann felt what Joseph Kniskern says in his book, *When the Vow Breaks:* (7)

> Divorce is as close as you can get to dying without actually dying. Only those who have experienced it can truly understand its dark power to test emotions and intellect to the ultimate degree.

Annette Dawson and her husband Lloyd had been married for eighteen years. Lloyd was a pastor of a developing church. Annette and Lloyd were dearly loved by their church. One afternoon, when Annette got home from work, she went upstairs to change her clothes before preparing supper. She noticed an envelope on her bed. It was a letter from her husband, saying that their marriage was over and that he had left. He told her not to come looking for him, but that he would call her in a few days. It turned out that Lloyd had left with his secretary. She, too, had written to her husband, telling him the same thing.

> **For out of the heart proceed evil thoughts, murders, adulteries, fornications, thefts, false witness, blasphemies.**
>
> **—Matthew 15:19**

Can one understand the mental and emotional damage from such an affair? This type of experience takes years to get over fully. Everyone loses in the two families. No one wins. Not only that, but there were teenagers in these two families. This makes the situation even more serious, as these young people are damaged for life.

A gifted lady, Sharon, who is fifty-six years old, put it this way when she got a divorce:

> My spouse suffered from an addiction to women. This was diagnosed in counseling. We worked on this problem in our marriage but he wasn't able to forgive himself.

There are workaholics who work more than is necessary. There are others who enjoy their work and do not mind putting in more hours than are required. However, sad to say, some spend more time at work for other reasons. Why is the spouse married to the workplace? Is it because the home is too negative? Too discouraging? Does the spouse feel unloved? Is it because the individual is spending time with someone else and is using the workplace as an excuse? Is the spouse suffering from a deep sense of inferiority? Is it an authentic call for help and the need is a matter of life and death? This is especially a problem with the medical profession, although others can experience this difficulty, too.

> **My time is as much mine as my money. If I don't let everyone else spend my money, I am not going to let them spend my time.**
>
> **—Fred Smith**

Dr. Paul Ambrose was on staff at a major women's hospital and faced emergencies at odd hours. However, there were other doctors on call, too.

After forty years of marriage, his wife Shirley walked out on him and sought a divorce. She simply got tired of fixing meals that were not eaten and of evening social events that were broken, due to his schedule. His grown daughter, Cheryl, shared with me how on her sixteenth birthday, a special event was planned by her mother. At the last moment, the phone rang and her father was called to do an emergency surgery. Cheryl felt that, for this special celebration, her father could have called upon another doctor. But he was so wrapped up in his sense of being a hero that he could not turn these calls down. Finally, after forty years of marriage, his wife just left.

> **For even when we were with you, this we commanded you, that if any would not work, neither should he eat.**
>
> **—2 Thessalonians 3:10**

In many ways, Dr. Ambrose's son, Paul, who became a prominent politician, took after his father and was always available when an individual in his community called upon him. He held his father in high esteem and followed his dad's example.

How many times have you heard this? What a tragedy when one is controlled by alcohol. Again, there are often issues that have led up to this. The important point is that, in the final analysis, alcohol led to the failure in the marriage. In addition, it touches the lives of all the family members and those closely related to the alcoholic.

**Wine is a mocker, strong drink is raging: and whosoever is deceived thereby is not wise.**
**—Proverbs 20:1**

Bill had a successful peanut and nut franchise. He was doing well until he started drinking on the job. He was in his eighteenth year of marriage when severe disagreements developed at home. He would stop at a local bar for happy hour and started drinking even more. At times, Shirley, his wife, would come looking for him and would drag him away. It was an unpleasant sight and a humbling experience. Bill did his best to hide bottles of alcohol in the garage, but Shirley knew where to look. It is very difficult for someone who does not drink to tolerate someone who does. Financial debts began to add up; and with reduced funds, things became critical. Finally, Shirley went back to work as a hairstylist to help make ends meet. This did not help Bill, as now he felt inadequate to provide for his family. Shirley continued to put her husband down. With her own income coming in, she became even more authoritative. It was too much for Bill to endure. The marriage was over. Thankfully, Bill started attending Alcoholics Anonymous, and before his death got his life turned around.

There are spouses who are well-organized and like to have things in place. There are other spouses who are messy and disorganized. If one is married to the other, you can appreciate the struggles that are sure to come. As one husband said about his wife:

> Sometimes, when I arrived home from work, I have had to shovel my way through the house. I do not understand how my wife can be so unorganized.

Cheryl is a forty-one-year old professor with a PhD in English. Her house is so messy that you wonder how she can find what she wants. Yet, you can ask her and she will pull out what she is looking for. Clothes from the washer are sitting on the dryer. The dining room table has a variety of items piled up on top of it! There are books, opened letters, and bills, along with a variety of clothes, all spread out on the furniture. Her dog is an important part of her house, and so he sits on her sofa and bed. With regards to her bed, it is usually unmade, except on the weekends. Her husband finally left her. He claimed he just got tired of living in such a messy house.

Some time ago, I was visiting the chairman of a large mission organization. His wife was a faculty member of a major university and held a PhD. The meeting was to be held in his home, which was located in one of the upscale areas of the city, where houses range from one million to ten million. Driving up to his home, one could see the special stone construction, the stained glass windows, and the impressive entrance. But what a disaster inside! There were books everywhere—in the living room, in the dining room, and in the kitchen, piled one on top of the other. There was no way anyone could use the dining room or kitchen table because of the books piled on them.

A pastor was sharing with me about an active member in his church, who complained about his wife's housekeeping. She was involved in the church to the point where some members called her the associate pastor, as she was there so many hours a week. The pastor, responding to her husband, went to their home one afternoon and was disgusted at the disarray of the furniture, the aroma, and the dust. He explained to the wife her husband's concern. It turned out that she did not like housework, including cleaning and organizing meals. The pastor helped save her marriage by encouraging her to reduce the amount of work and time she spent at the church and to increase her time at home. She came to appreciate Proverbs 14:1a:

> Every wise woman buildeth her own house.

If you go by statistics, you will find that in-laws account for one of three main reasons for the breakup of a marriage. This is hard to accept when you realize that parents want the best for their offspring. However, parents would like to have some say in the person their son or daughter is going to marry. No, it does not necessarily mean that they give outright approval by saying so, but in the quiet, perhaps disapproving, way they have relationships with the couple. There is that appearance of let us wait and see how it turns out.

More than one mother has said about her sons: *No girl is good enough for my boys!* The tragic reality is that many mothers really believe it. Right away, there are tensions and struggles between the wife and her mother-in-law. In the end, usually the wife wins, but at such a price! The time has come for parents to accept the fact that in marriage their children must leave the parents and start a new family unit.

**Therefore shall a man leave his father and mother, and shall cleave unto his wife: and they shall be one flesh.**
**—Genesis 2:24**

One young bride in my acquaintance married into a family where the mother was really "The Boss." The young bride, just after returning from her honeymoon, and wanting to impress her in-laws, invited them over for Sunday dinner. The mother-in-law said that the forks were on the wrong side of the plate and so raised her voice and said to her scared daughter-in-law: "This will not do for my son." She immediately corrected the place setting, but in doing so, greatly upset her daughter-in-law, who was now on pins and needles, not knowing what was coming next. Now in a case like this, her young husband should have spoken up in support of his wife, but he said nothing and let it pass. The young husband lost a great opportunity to show support for his wife and to indicate to his mother that he was now on his own.

In another situation with a different couple, the bride did not accept negative criticism from her mother-in-law, and told her new husband what she had heard about his mother. Well, the cloud broke and loosed a storm. The mother-in-law misunderstood that her new daughter-in-law was trying to defend her honor and tried to rebuke her daughter-in-law, who in turn confronted her mother-in-law. Before long, the mother was crying and left the house. Her other son, who was not at the gathering, heard what had happened and complained to his new sister-in-law to complain about how she had handled his mother. To make matters worse, the young husband joined forces with his brother. Well, there was no way the marriage could last. Again, the husband should have stood by his wife.

A young couple must bear in mind that their former relational family styles might not work as they blend their lives together. Most likely, they will form their own identity, which, if not acceptable, can lead to a breakup of the marriage, as well as cause conflict with the in-laws. This leads to the conclusion that relationships with the in-laws should be taken seriously. Be careful that your marriage is not threatened by them.

Many couples enter marriage ignorant of what they are getting into. They fail to realize that marriage is a legal contract and that there are consequences if you simply walk out of it. Neither Cheryl Roberts, a forty-four-year old lady, nor her husband, Cecil, really understood what they were doing when they married. This is what she wrote about her failed marriage:

> After many years of studying, researching and pondering as to why my marriage failed, I believe the failure was due largely to ignorance about what makes a successful relationship. Our marriage was like taking a trip around the world without a map. We would get lost if we didn't seek direction.
>
> I thought my husband and I would be happily married forever, because we had lots of fun together. However, neither of us had learned that a happy and successful marriage required skill and commitment. We didn't know that it was normal for marriages to go through hard times and that, with the right attitude, heart, and commitment, we would be back on track. We didn't know how to be loving persons.
>
> My husband left me after thirty years of marriage. He made this bad choice from a depressed posture and soon discovered that he was not happy anywhere. I don't blame my husband for destroying our marriage. I feel our society has failed us. Our society teaches us so many useful things, but no how-to's on being a loving person and a good marriage partner. We live in a disposable society, where we throw everything out when we have used it up, including relationships.
>
> If I were to marry again, I would want my partner to be living a Christian life, practicing Christian principles, and following the Lord, not his own feelings and judgments. I want a partner who knows that the Bible is the truth and that we need the Lord to make all our decisions. I want a partner who has been transformed through Christ

to a character of honesty, integrity, and commitment to marriage and family, not to his own self-centeredness. I want a partner who has learned how to communicate, solve problems in a Christian way, and who will be open and honest with me and seek Christian counsel when confused.

I must keep reminding myself that I also must be the right person in order to meet my partner's needs, by following the Lord and Christian principles, as it takes two emotionally healthy people to make a successful marriage.

Money makes the world go 'round, and finances play a significant role in marriage. Although money might not be the major component in the break-up of a marriage, it could well be a factor.

**The love of money is the root of all evil.**
**—1 Timothy 6:10**

Joyce Bradley was in a financial jam when she invited us to look at her monetary situation. She was being forced to sell her house, which she did not want to do. She owed $25,000 on credit cards. She was only able to pay the minimum each month, although when an offer came through to secure a new card with a lower interest rate for six months, she latched on to it. In addition, she had mortgage payments, a daughter in university, and other bills. I felt sorry for her, until she informed me that her salary was $133,000. She had lived alone since her divorce from her husband. The two spent their combined income of $250,000 and had no savings. This was one issue that led to the breakup of their marriage. Her home was average and her expenses were reasonable. However, she found ways and means to exhaust her income.

Thirty-nine-year old Judith Peters, who taught at a major university, had a remuneration exceeding $200,000, but very little to show for it. When people who handle money poorly enter marriage, one can understand why finances would be a problem.

Every couple should know how to draw up a budget and stick with it. If their credit cards are not paid off monthly, they should cease using them! My friend Linda Black asked if I would help her with her finances. It took very little time to draw up a budget, at which time we discovered that her monthly disbursements exceeded her remuneration. This led to some tough decisions to bring one into line with the other. For example, she enjoys eating out (for that matter, we all do). But if you are limited in your budget, you have to forego some of the things you like to do.

The Crown Financial Course is an excellent tool to help couples get off to a sound financial pathway for life.

There is an old saying that some people use when they are courting:

Prove your love to me by going to bed with me.

Actually, real love is expressed when we protect and respect the one being courted. Many times, when one has yielded, the aggressor shuns the other and simply walks away. In reality, men enjoy the individual who stands her ground and insists on waiting for her wedding day.

**Marriage is honourable in all, and the bed undefiled.**
**—Hebrews 13:4a**

Pre-marital sex can lead to a guilty conscience in marriage. Mel and his wife Janet were having serious marital problems. They were confused and could not understand why they were constantly arguing. I discovered that their firstborn was conceived before they were married. They asked God to forgive them, but really never accepted that forgiveness, even though they prayed several times. After assuring them of complete forgiveness by God, they were at peace with one another and divorce was set aside. Those who do not wait for their honeymoon really lose out on the excitement of exploring together this God-given gift of sexuality.

Dorothy Roberts married her beloved John, only to discover that he had herpes. He confessed to having dated several ladies, four of whom he had had sex with. Dorothy sought out a counselor, who advised her to have her doctor examine her and also her husband immediately.

A lady is blessed indeed when her lover treats her body as the temple of God.

Domestic violence is much more widespread than reported. It includes physical, emotional, and sexual abuse. It touches the lives of the abused and their family members. Physical abuse usually is carried out by the husband because he is stronger, but once in a while I have met a wife who was the abuser. Physical abuse can involve hitting, shoving, kicking, choking, throwing objects, or using a weapon.

> **To be angry with the right person, to the right extent, at the right time, with the right object and in the right way—it is not everyone who can do it.**
>
> **—Aristotle**

It was Saturday morning around 9:30 when Andy Small came to my office at church. He was a depressed individual, whose red eyes indicated that he was on the verge of crying. The story was sad indeed. He had lost his temper and dragged his wife from the living room to the bedroom, where he had hit her again and again. She did not call the police. This type of violence is widespread and must not be tolerated. Yes, the abuser may apologize and make promises that it will never happen again, but it usually does. These offenders should be forced to take a course on anger management. Without a solution to the underlying anger issue, physical abuse likely will occur again within the next six to eight weeks.

Jane is a forty-four-year old lady who works for Bell Telephone. Her partner would take the liberty of physically abusing her if anything went wrong. He would tell her that she was always to blame. The point came when she could no longer trust him. Finally, she said to him:

> Look, you don't really love me, and I do not love you, so let's go our separate ways.

It has been suggested that the first time a husband physically abuses his wife, she needs to face reality and get a legal restraining order. In this way, he will either straighten up or lose his family. This means financial problems for her, but they will come later on if she waits.

Can you imagine what it would be like to live with a spouse who is bipolar? Manic depression has led to the breakup of families and severe issues for spouses and children. It can strike people of all ages and occupations. A bipolar individual experiences real mood swings, and this has divided families, jeopardized careers, and done great emotional damage to many people. There are three sources of depression: physical illness, a situational depression, and a biochemical disorder.

> **Love, hope, fear, faith—these make humanity; these are its signs, its note, and character.**
>
> **—Joseph Butler**

Hal Anderson was a successful realtor in a community of one hundred thousand. At times, he worked day and night. He also served as superintendent of the church Sunday school. He drove the teachers to reach out and enlarge their classes. It was one promotional drive after another. Nothing could please him, although record goals were reached and passed. At other times, Hal would slow down and little would take place. He would become quite critical at times. This went on for several years. One night, Hal did not show up at home, and so early the next morning, his wife, Lois, called the police. Sadly, they found him in the church parking lot with a rubber tube from the exhaust leading into the car. He had been dead for several hours.

Wilma Noaks, a sixty-nine-year old senior, went on a European cruise with Nancy Peel. The two got along really well. One morning, Wilma felt so good she decided not to take her pill for the day. The next morning, she felt tired and wished to sleep in. On a number of days, Nancy had to see to it that Wilma took her pills. Upon returning home from Europe, Wilma did not take her pills and, arriving at Nancy's house, was acting strangely. Her husband, Ron, came and picked her up. Early the next morning, Ron had to take her to the hospital. Returning home from the hospital, Wilma helped with the farm and did so for the next ten weeks. Ron kept an eye on his wife and sought to have her by his side all the time.

One morning, Ron had to get something and told Wilma he would be right back. Quickly, Wilma went for the car key only to discover that Ron had taken it. Her son's car was there so she went into his room, took his car key, and drove off. When Ron got back, he found his wife missing and immediately went looking for her. Taking some helpers, he found his son's car by a nearby lake. Wilma's body was discovered in the lake where she had taken her life.

"You can have the real thing instead of a picture model," one wife said to her husband, who was looking at pornography. More and more marriages are breaking up due to this distasteful sexual perversion. Profit makers have taken the God-given gift of sex and made cheap videos that are ruining many marriages and corrupting our youth in their formative years. Recent statistics indicate that one third of all men are engaged in pornography. It would appear that this is happening even amongst Christians. This is shocking, as it defeats one of the reasons why God has given us this precious gift of sex. In addition, those who are engaged in pornography are indicating that either their spouse is not meeting their needs or they are not satisfied with their spouse!

Pornography also degrades the mind. The brain is like a computer—the pictures enter the mind, but how does one erase what they have seen? At least with the computer, you can delete it.

John Miner was pastor of a small church. He and his wife, Mary, were having domestic problems connected with intimacy. John suggested they rent a couple of pornography videos. Mary did not like this, but decided that if it would help keep their marriage together, she would agree. You can imagine what the result was. Mary was disgusted by the videos and ashamed that she had gone along with it. Their marriage broke up and so did John's work in the ministry.

Vicky Brant, a fifty-eight-year old woman, got a phone call from a friend at her bank, who informed her that Gary, her husband, had just withdrawn a large sum of money. That night, after supper, Vicky went up to their home office to discuss why such a large sum had been withdrawn. She found Gary looking at pornography. He admitted to his addiction, but refused to get help. Within a few months their marriage broke up!

While many blended families have worked out well, many have not! Seeking to blend two families, in which there are children, can be a challenge. In some families, there are children from one spouse, while in others, there are children from both spouses. In still others, there are children from both spouses' previous marriages, as well as those they have had together. The situation gets even more complex when there are children from two former spouses, making for three or even four sets of children now living under one roof.

> **There is nothing you can give your children that will be more lasting or more deeply appreciated than the gift of yourself.**
>
> **—Richard Exley**

Perhaps the number one factor that can cause problems in blended families is the area of discipline. From the first day, the couple needs to agree on how to handle the misbehavior of the children. Neil, a thirty-five-year old father whose stepfamily included five of his own children from a previous marriage plus two stepchildren, wisely suggested in his book *The Second Time Around* that both spouses need to think through how they want to apply discipline and who should involved. He further suggests that the rules be written down so that there can be no misunderstanding. (163)

Two interesting factors in Neil's book are: be sure to include rewards for good behavior and have the step-parent participate in applying both discipline and rewards.

Being consistent is one of the more difficult things to practice, but it is so important. Children will test the parent at first to see if he or she will carry through with what has been said. It is most important that the one spouse should support the other in front of the children. It is not difficult to understand that when only one of the spouses has had children, complex problems can arise, resulting in the childless spouse giving up and walking away from the marriage. It takes considerable patience for a childless adult to marry a spouse with children who are still growing up.

There are some people who develop emotionally, physically, and mentally more slowly than others. On the other hand, one may marry a partner who is underage chronologically for marriage.

**In real love, you want the other person's good. In romantic love, you want the other person.**
**—Margaret C. Anderson**

Dorothy Johnson was a clever student in school. She started kindergarten at the age of four and was advanced one year in elementary school. She started high school the youngest in her class. As a result, her school friends were two and three years older than herself. A number of her school friends started marrying when they were between eighteen and twenty years of age.

Jack Peterson, who was dating Dorothy, suggested marriage. She was pleased to keep up with her friends. She had no marital counseling and had not dated anyone else besides Jack. Although Dorothy's parents thought sixteen was too young to marry, they agreed and gave her a beautiful wedding. Within a matter of weeks, Jack and Dorothy began to have problems. Dorothy, raised in a middle class family, was accustomed to new clothes and eating out once a week. Jack, raised by a single mom, had limited means. In fact, Jack's mother had problems making ends meet. She often purchased clothes from the Salvation Army thrift store. Jack had a low-paying job.

To add to their domestic problems, Dorothy became pregnant in their first year of marriage. Yes, her parents tried to help her financially, but Jack objected to this. To make matters worse, at the beginning of their second year of marriage, their car broke down. Because Jack had a job that required a car, the couple went into serious financial debt. Other financial complications arose and the couple drifted apart, eventually filing for bankruptcy. Dorothy, now twenty years of age, was unable to handle the domestic scene emotionally, and so their marriage ended.

Some people can become so addicted to the television, watching soaps series, the news, and information programs, that they neglect their daily routine of chores and responsibilities. Laziness sets in unnoticed and causes problems with spousal relationships. One frustrated housewife said:

> It takes no initiative to do anything. I will get around to it.

For years, Jan Ferguson carried on a fine gardening business. She worked long hours, but it paid off. At the age of sixty, she decided to retire and take things at a slower pace. After breakfast she would turn on the television and watch *General Hospital, Guiding Light,* and other interesting stories. One day was spent in this manner and then the next.

> **I find television very educating. Every time somebody turns on the set, I go into the other room and read a book.**
>
> **—Groucho Marx**

The dishes began to pile up in the sink. Beds were now unmade and the rugs were no longer vacuumed. Supper started to be served late. One thing led to the other until Anthony, her husband, started to complain. Arguments followed and many negative remarks were made by both of them. Jean was unable to get away from the soap series. Finally, they separated and the marriage was over. One can appreciate Proverbs 12:27a:

> The slothful [lazy] man roasteth not that which he took in hunting.

Some Christian men have taken Ephesians five, where Paul talks about the mystical union between Christ and the church, as meaning that the husband is "The Boss" over his wife. Some husbands take the phrase from Ephesians,

Wives, submit to your husbands in everything,

to mean that they can order their wives around like a commander in chief. We have met husbands like that, and we feel very sorry for the wives in such a union. An overly controlling spouse can wreck a marriage easily. Not only does the dictator rule his wife with an iron hand, but his children as well. In many of these families, sons follow the negative example of the father and marry with the spirit of domination.

I remember so well a police officer, active in the church, who was "The Boss" in his family. He controlled his wife and children like a dictator. He kept charge of their schedules, finances, and friends. Later, when the teens started to date, he had to approve their dates and schedules. As a police officer, he served justice in his own way, and no one in the family dared question him. His was not a happy family, and it was difficult to minister to their spiritual needs. An interesting comment was made by one wife raised in such a situation. In her own words:

I find it hard to pray to God as my Father, as my own father was so hard on us.

This is a heartbreaker, as the woman's husband also was a dictator. Somehow in the courting process she failed to notice his tendency to dominate.

How can a wife handle such a situation without getting a divorce? This is where prayer and patience come into the picture. When the moment is right, she should speak to that dictatorial husband and explain how his behavior is hurting the relationships within the family. Furthermore, she should ask if he would be willing to go with her to a counselor to discuss saving the marriage. If in the process he gives her a punch, that is the time to call the police.

Some marriages have grown stale. The marriage is neither cold nor hot. There is very little excitement, and the husband and wife take each other for granted. They have failed to bring into their relationship surprise or evidence of their appreciation for and commitment to each other. The one word that best describes their home is monotonous.

Seldom do they get out to eat or have relatives or friends in for an evening. The phone rings from time to time, but they refuse to respond to invitations to outside activities. They are, for the most part, left to themselves; and although they do not like it, they make no effort to change their circumstances. They are trapped in their marriage, so to speak, and do not exercise the energy needed to get out from under the burden. They are followers, not leaders.

Mary Gates was a cashier working in a supersize grocery store. She put in her eight-hour shift and went straight home afterward. She even turned down the annual Christmas party for fear of having to socialize. She was called a *loner* by her fellow workers.

Her husband, Hugh Gates, was a tool and dye maker employed by a firm that makes parts for General Motors. Very much like his wife, he, too, kept to himself and did little socializing. He was shy and did not like to mix with others.

Hugh and Mary had three children, and all of them were married by the age of twenty-two. When they became empty nesters, it soon became apparent that they had little to offer each other, and the problem grew to serious proportions. It did not occur to them, before it was too late, that everything in life is tied into relationships.

**A woman ran an ad in the classifieds: "Husband wanted." Next day, she received a hundred letters. They all said the same thing: "You can have mine."**
**—Unknown**

Where was the church to assist them? Well, the church was there, and the one they attended had over a dozen small group meetings. But you cannot force the issue; Hugh and Mary went in and out, going through the motions of being good people without applying what the pastor was teaching. Hugh and Mary decided to go their own separate ways, with divorce being the probable end result. Their pastor heard about it and made arrangements to see them together. The story has a happy ending: Hugh and Mary got involved with several other couples in their fifties. Here they heard about other couples with problems and how they handled them.

They came to appreciate Ecclesiastes 4:9a: "Two are better than one." Hugh was moved when his group read Proverbs 18:22a: "Whoso findeth a wife, findeth a good thing." The study that night focused on marriage relationships, and it became very meaningful to Hugh and Mary. And so the marriage was saved.

Gurneet Singh was forty-two when she spoke to us about her marriage. Now residing in North America, she went home to visit her parents in India. Her parents had picked out what they thought was a suitable man for their daughter. Actually, they had three in mind, but Gurneet would have nothing to do with two of them. She had questions about the third, but decided to obey her parents as they surely would know what was best. The marriage was a disaster. It turned out that the bridegroom only wanted a wife as someone to sponsor him to come to North America. After getting here, he was soon gone and the parents regretted the whole affair.

> **Divorce is very much like death with one notable difference. When a spouse dies, he or she is dead and gone. When a couple divorces, the relationship is dead, love is dead, the marriage is dead, but the spouse is very much alive.**
>
> **—Richard Exley**

Now, Gurneet was a married woman but forsaken! Who would want to marry her now, especially someone from her own culture and background? This left her no choice but to get a divorce as soon as possible. Fortunately, she was an accomplished and desirable woman. She joined the church choir and became very sociable. Gurneet did not limit her dating to Asians, but felt at home with men from other cultures as well.

I am sure that many arranged marriages have been most successful, especially when the parents did their homework and secured a likely bridegroom who would be a blessing to their daughter.

Norma McKee cannot remember her parents, because she was raised by her aunt from infancy. Her aunt and uncle did what they could to raise her, along with their own children, but finances were limited when Norma was growing up. There were the usual family disputes, and Norma was not treated as an equal. Things did not improve when Norma got into her teen years. Actually, she was just waiting for her sixteenth birthday, when she thought she could perhaps get out on her own.

It was natural for Norma to begin dating Keith Barry when he came on the scene. Within a short order, he started talking about marriage. They were heavily involved in sex. Why not accept Keith and get out from the burden of the home situation, she thought to herself. In a very short time, Norma realized that she had gone from the frying pan into the fire! She was now well along with her first pregnancy. After several failed marriages and a few more pregnancies, she realized that she did not know how to relate to men, except by sex. Years later, her life was changed when she shifted her focus from self to God.

A common mistake in remarrying is to speed up the marriage ceremony. After all, it is not like getting married for the first time. The honeymoon experience will be a rerun! In fact, the marriage will be the same! The individual will soon discover that things are not the same at all, except the mistakes made in the first will most likely be repeated in the second.

It takes time to recover fully from divorce or the death of a spouse. This is true especially in the case of a divorced person. Forgiving your ex-spouse takes time, really and truly letting the past be the past. It may well be that your ex was largely to blame for the break-down of the marriage, but perhaps you had a small part in it, too, and if so, have you learned from it?

> **What are you looking for in a mate? Someone who won't divorce me!**
> **—Florida man, 56, married three times**

It would appear that older men who lose their spouse by death are more likely to remarry rather than to live alone. It is harder for a man to live alone than for a woman. Men are not as familiar with cleaning, shopping, and meal preparation, and soon want to change things by finding a suitable wife.

It should be noted that there is an ample supply of available women for marriage, much more so than for men who are available! This is where time is an important factor before jumping into marriage again.

Of course, it is not that much of a problem for an available lady to invite a man for coffee or home for lunch. A tasty hot dish, with a salad and a great dessert, topped off with a lighted candle, and he sees what life could be like with her.

The problem is that life is much more than a tasty lunch and beautifully set table! There are so many things to take into consideration before one takes the walk to the marriage altar. We are looking at marrying too soon. There have been situations where the divorce has been granted and the next day one of the party members announces their engagement. Very little time has been spent getting to know the partner and to confirm that the two are ready for marriage. Many trained counselors suggest that you take a period of twenty-four months before remarriage after the death or divorce of a spouse.

Why do people marry? Some do for the wrong reason. Yes, there are those who marry for money. Just think of the things that could be purchased, the car I will be able to drive, the clothes I will wear. Many of these folks were raised with little to spare, and now see an opportunity to change their physical circumstances. What will it be like if the stock market goes down and they lose much of what they have?

> **Once you're in the throes of a relationship, logic does go out the window and you can only see what you want to see.**
>
> **—Edward Tauber**

Others marry because of the position being held by their future marriage partner. It may be one in politics or one in his company. Just think of the prestige of being married to such an individual. One could make a lot of people jealous and get some revenge on those who used to look down on them. The problem arises when the material circumstances change.

Others marry for chemistry. The exciting moments around him or her will only last for a time. What happens when things return to normal? It is at such a time that character becomes more meaningful than reputation.

People finally come to realize that a marriage must be built on love, steadfastness, and an earnest desire to serve your spouse.

People do differ in the development of personal intelligence and mental alertness. Perhaps at their wedding they are somewhat even. However, after marriage, one may be involved in a work that commands creative thinking, planning, and reading. The other spouse might not be interested in reading or personal development. The couple soon may begin to pull apart and before long are strangers to each other.

**Life is what we make it, always has been, always will be.**

**—Grandma Moses**

In one marriage, the wife was raised with classical music and attended great concerts. She married a man who never was taken to concerts or exposed to some of the finer things of life. So to speak, she married below herself. Unless she exercises patience and longsuffering, and, bit by bit, seeks to bring him up closer to her level, there will be problems. It is important that the husband and the wife grow together in developing their mental alertness and intelligence.

As I was writing, my telephone rang. It was Pam Smith, who married five years ago. Pam asked one of her friends to do the service. Her call today dealt with domestic problems she was experiencing with her husband. She did not really know her husband before their marriage. Since the wedding, it appears that he only has wanted her money and that he has quite a temper. She found out, with many others, that it takes time to know someone. Now she regrets the marriage. How could this have happened?

Well for one thing, the courtship was too short. She realizes now that it was not long enough, but at the time, she was concerned to get the marriage official before someone else went after him. This in itself should have told her that they were not ready for marriage. As she said, "He is such a nice looking gentleman, and besides, he took care of his sick wife for two years until she died." However, she did not know for sure that the things he told her were true! It takes more than six months to get to know the one you are planning to marry.

Another problem is that Pam did not discuss some of the vital issues of a relationship before they married. How were they going to handle money? She was bringing into the marriage twice the cash he had. Nor had they discussed their habits and traditions. Here they had to compromise, but their attitudes were not apt for this. The last word he said to Pam was, "See you in court!" What a pity that this should happen to people in their sixties!

Consider how much negative baggage two divorced people bring into their remarriage! Let us imagine the husband is in his late sixties and the wife in her late fifties. She is accustomed to sleeping through the night while he, due to his prostate, has to get up three or four times. He likes to golf every Saturday with the boys, but she wants him to do something with her on Saturdays.

She brings into the marriage three children, but he never had a family. Can you picture the negative factors that will appear almost immediately? It is not easy to maintain a good marriage unless these things have been discussed and agree upon earlier.

Another serious problem is if the husband has ongoing monthly support payments for his first family. What happens if he loses his job and the money is not there? Does the new family suffer? Unless the two can be reasonable and compromise, there will be problems on how best to handle negative baggage.

**Each day is a new life. Seize it. Live it. For in today already walks tomorrow.**

**—David Guy Powers**

Just because there is considerable negative baggage, it does not mean you should not marry; but these things need to be brought out into the open and discussed.

# Wrap Up

These are twenty-five issues that can lead to the breakup of a marriage. You can probably think of others. For those planning on marriage and for those of us who are already married, we would do well to understand how and why some marriages fail.

# Think About This!

---

In your judgment, what are the three most important issues that can break up a marriage?

......................................................................................................................

......................................................................................................................

......................................................................................................................

And what can one do to avoid such a situation?

......................................................................................................................

......................................................................................................................

......................................................................................................................

......................................................................................................................

......................................................................................................................

......................................................................................................................

......................................................................................................................

......................................................................................................................

......................................................................................................................

......................................................................................................................

......................................................................................................................

......................................................................................................................

......................................................................................................................

......................................................................................................................

......................................................................................................................

# CHAPTER THREE

# Be the Right Person to Marry
# the Right Person

Being the right person means a better opportunity for marrying the right person. However, it is difficult to marry the right person if we ourselves are not living up to what we expect from a spouse. This leads us to name what we would like to see in the one we marry. If we are going to know, to some degree, the person to whom we are pledging the rest of our days, a courtship of at least a year is a necessity. At the same time, it clearly is impossible to know all that we desire to know about an individual until we are married.

**You don't get to choose how you're going to die or when. You can only decide how you're going to live.**
**—Joan Baez**

It seems to me that some people spend more time shopping for a car than they do considering a potential spouse. Over the past five years, several couples have talked to me about their approaching marriage. When asked how long they have known each other, the answer often has been, "Well, we met on the Internet five or six weeks ago!" Time after time, the marriage did not work out because of personal issues that did not surface on the Internet. The following are foundational to a solid and happy marriage.

It is true that at times opposites attract, but when it comes to spiritual matters, it is imperative that a couple has as much in common as possible. The Bible is very clear that a Christian believer should only marry another Christian believer.

> **Be ye not unequally yoked together with unbelievers: for what fellowship hath righteousness with unrighteousness?**
> **—2 Corinthians 6:14a**

Several times over the years, a Christian has told me that their fiancé is a good person and shares the same values. Or they will say that he or she has assured them that they will not stop them from going to church. Or, in several cases there has been a quick conversion, only to find out later that it was not genuine. It is a mistake to expect a person to change after they are married!

Besides being one in faith, it is best when both members of the marriage have the same spiritual commitment. It is a powerful testimony to the world when a couple has dedicated their home to the glory of God, where the Bible is read and where the name of Jesus Christ is honored!

Blessed is that home where around the breakfast or dinner table, the Bible is open, a page from a devotional book is read, and prayers are offered. In many homes, the family practices what is called "Conversational Prayer." This is where one family member opens and another adds to the prayer. It makes for a fine spirit of communion with the Lord.

This high level of spiritual commitment needs to start when a couple begins seriously dating. A number of deeply committed men have asked the Lord to bless them as they were dating their future spouses. This means so much to a lady who has an earnest desire to honor Jesus Christ in her life.

Is there any better way to raise children than in a home where Jesus Christ is exalted and where love is so evident? Begin to look and expect to find a spouse who has been born again and has a deep desire to glorify God.

You know the three T's of generosity: Time! Talent! Treasury! Is my potential spouse giving of their time to serve the Lord? We are asked to give a tenth of our money to the Lord, but what about tithing our time? There are so many opportunities to serve others, and in doing so, we are serving our Lord. A seventy-two-year old man drives patients from a small community to a major hospital for cancer treatments one afternoon a week. A seventy-eight-year old lady reads to the blind every Thursday afternoon. A fifty-one-year old accountant helps seniors with their home accounting. A forty-four-year old surgeon gives a week every quarter to serve people in Africa. There are multiple opportunities for one to give time to serve others, and consequently the Lord Jesus Christ. Observe if your potential spouse does volunteer work. As you spend time courting one another, take note how and where he or she is serving.

> **I expect to pass through this world but once. Any good therefore I can do, or any kindness I can show to my fellow creatures, let me do it now. Let me not defer or neglect it, for I shall not pass this way again.**
> **—Stephen Grellet**

Talent is another fine way by which to show your generosity. Take time to prepare for the Sunday services; pray and seek God's guidance as to how you can best use your talent, whether it is in teaching or in the area of music. Your local church provides many opportunities to use your talent to good advantage. Again, observe the talent of your friend and see how generously it is being used.

> **Our deeds still travel with us from afar. And what we have been makes us what we are.**
> **—George Eliot**

Treasury is what instantly comes to our minds when we think of generosity. Money and our use of it is a surefire indicator of our dedication to God. It is wise to discuss this issue while you are dating. If you become serious about each other, why not exchange your last year's tax returns? This gives a clear picture of how you each handle your charitable giving. You will be doing this when married, so why not also before the wedding?

Reputation is what others believe you to be. Character is what you are when you are alone. Chemistry is what attracts you to an individual, but character is what keeps you with him or her. What are some of the traits to look for in determining someone's character?

**My parents taught me through deed, not just word, perhaps the most important of life's character lessons: character trumps genius.**

**—Pamela Wallin**

Integrity is an important aspect of one's character. Does your friend keep promises? Are they always honest when dealing with monetary issues? One lady observed that when her gentleman went to pay the dinner bill, he noticed that the dessert expense was missing. He drew it to the attention of the cashier, who was most grateful for his honesty. She was quite taken with this display of integrity. It was not the last time he showed his honesty. Thus, when he proposed, she accepted immediately. She sensed that she had found a man she could trust.

Dependability is another aspect of character . . . being on time and following through in what you said you would do. These can be observed while you are courting.

Does your potential spouse tend to anticipate the best possible outcome? In other words, is the bottle half-filled or half-empty? There are some folks who never see the light of day, but live with a constantly negative outlook on life. To them, there is very little that is good and upright. Things do not function, according to them, effectively. These folks are subject to depression and tend to be pessimistic. Regardless of what you say or do, things just do not turn out the way you intended.

I have been working with one individual who does not have a positive outlook in most everything. No matter what one says, it just cannot be so. This individual has such low self-esteem. You give them a sincere compliment, and it is turned around to something negative. This is a fairly easy character trait to pick out when courting. Unless you want to face a continual stream of negative remarks, it would be wise to reconsider the individual as a potential mate, unless you already have a deep love for them and are ready to exercise much patience in marriage.

One way to help a pessimist is to point out the providence of God in our lives. As we read in Psalm 90:15,

> Make us glad according to the days wherein thou hast
> afflicted us, and the years wherein we have seen evil.

It is great to realize that God overrules in our lives and that everything has a purpose. Encourage the pessimist to turn their eyes to the God of providence, which might help them to move from a depressed spirit to a more forward-thinking attitude.

In this day of commerce, when it is seen as normal to gather "stuff" day after day until our closets are overflowing, it is easy to develop a selfish spirit. We must have this! We must have that! Before you know it, a self-centered attitude may develop.

**He who falls in love with himself will have no rivals.**
**—Benjamin Franklin**

What is the answer? Anyone considering marriage must think of the implications. It is no longer "I," but "we." How do you know when both of you have made the switch? By the way suggestions and decisions are made.

Do you and your friend ask each other:

> What would you like to do?
> Where would you like to go for dinner?
> What would you like to watch?

In other words, an unselfish individual is more concerned about the other person and their needs. This too can be discerned in your courting period.

This sounds negative, but actually it is a positive trait. Smoking is the leading cause for throat cancer today, according to a cancer surgeon. He says that at least eighty percent of throat cancer cases can be traced back to the smoking of tobacco. It is very hard for a non-smoker to live with a smoker. It really is a dirty habit. The smell gets into furniture and clothing. In addition, it is a habit that directly and negatively affects those living with the smoker.

Money may not be a problem for you, but many smokers will spend from three hundred to six hundred dollars a year, on tobacco. What a waste! Generally, smokers will throw their butts on the street. This means that the municipality must spend money to pick them up. While writing this, I heard that the city of San Francisco is planning to place a thirty-five cent tax on each carton of cigarettes to help pay for picking up the butts. It would appear to me that this tax may soon be copied throughout North America, and well it should be! It is a disgusting thing to see smokers throw their butts on sidewalks, alleys, and roadways.

You have the classic Word of God in Genesis 2:24, 25:

> Therefore shall a man leave his father and his mother, and shall cleave unto his wife: and they shall be one flesh. And they were both naked, the man and his wife, and were not ashamed.

Getting married involves leaving home, relatives, and, yes, at times, friends. Why? Your spouse has become number one in your life. The two of you are now dependent on each other. This does not lessen your respect and love for your parents. It is simply an acknowledgement that you have formed a new unit in society, and that union takes first place, even over the parents. Mature parents, wanting the best for their married children, accept and recognize this and are careful not to interfere.

One married daughter, after having a serious dispute with her husband, called her father and asked if she could come home. He replied:

> My dear daughter, you are home. Think of what you have
> and be grateful.

Of course, if the daughter had been in physical danger, her father would have responded differently. Most couples will have their own misunderstandings, and as such, they must work them out together as a couple.

This aspect of your spouse being number one also includes recreation, work, hobbies, and other interests. Does that mean one must give up things that are personally enjoyable? No, but it does mean that your spouse is given first place, if the time comes to choose between working on a hobby and doing something together.

Happiness is manifested in many ways. Do I really enjoy living? Is it my aspiration to make my spouse happy? What steps will I need to take to spread happiness to others? The Bible gives clear direction for the development of a happy heart. In Psalm 1, we read about how we should walk. In Psalm 97:11, we are reminded that gladness comes for those who are upright in heart. In Matthew 5, our Lord gives a prescription for happiness in what are known as The Beatitudes. And Paul, in his letter to the church in Philippi, mentions joy some thirteen times.

> **Many persons have a wrong idea of what constitutes true happiness. It is not attained through self-gratification but through fidelity to a worthy purpose.**
>
> **—Helen Keller**

No, it is not smiling all day long or displaying an over-abounding joy, but a deep satisfaction of the heart. It manifests itself in being contented and grateful for the gift of life. Happiness does not come from the collecting of things such as cars, boats, and clothes. Happiness is a result of positive relationships with others. So look for one who knows how to get along with others.

> **A happy person is not a person in a certain set of circumstances, but rather a person with a certain set of attitudes.**
>
> **—Hugh Downs**

Happiness begins early in life. Perhaps you know the story of Wilfrid Laurier, a former prime minister of Canada. Gordon Donaldson shares the following in his book *Eighteen Men:*

> Wilfred Laurier grew up in a poverty- stricken home. He slept on a narrow shelf in a closet of the cramped little house, but he considered himself well-off. There was fishing in the summer, and woods and streams to explore. In the winter there were books. Laurier had a happy home followed by a happy marriage. There was about him a shininess of soul that brightened his time.

Quiet time for reflection, Bible reading, and prayer will give your day a quality of living that satisfies the soul. It is best if the husband takes the lead. It is easier for the wife to follow her husband than for a husband to follow his wife, in things of the Spirit.

**Let the word of Christ dwell in you richly.**
**—Colossians 3:16**

In our home, for years, we take time, usually at the breakfast table, to read a portion of Scripture, while my wife will read from a devotional guide. This has become a daily routine and one that really delights us. This emphasis on the spiritual also includes Sunday worship, which we faithfully attend. This honors our God but it also gives us the opportunity to associate with friends of long-standing. This emphasis on the spiritual also includes our pocketbook, where we set aside, weekly, a portion of what we have received. It includes revenue from all sources.

It is amazing how many books we have read in our daily quiet time. At present, we are being blessed with the writings of Vance Havner. Before that, we enjoyed two books by Anne Graham Lotz. For two years we used a book published by Nelson on church history, *The One Year Book on Church History*. We like to close the day with a devotional guide, followed by prayer. It is a fine way to fall asleep, with godly thoughts on your mind. But it takes time. You must include it as part of your day, and, yes, make it a priority.

Are you amazed at how little things can have an impact on your relationships? While driving on the highway, reach over and touch your spouse. It communicates that you are thinking of them. Husbands, bring a potted plant or a bouquet of flowers home to your wife. She will probably ask you what you have been up to. But do it anyway! And wives, on occasion, prepare his favorite dessert. He will love you for it. Leave little notes for your spouse where he or she will find them. Think of different things to say. I heard or read the following:

You know what I like about you? Everything!

You see, your spouse is special. You have chosen your spouse out of all the people in the world. Yes, to you, your spouse is number one! And remind him or her of this time and time again by your actions.

Have there been times when in the late afternoon your wife says she is tired? This is your opportunity to suggest that the two of you have dinner out so she does not have to prepare it.

Have there been times when you were going to go out for the evening and your spouse said, "Do we have to go out tonight?" This is your opportunity to suggest that you stay home, relax, and read.

**One of the uncomfortable facts about ourselves is that we all must live in a way that meets our own approval.**
**—Paul Holmer**

It is important, over the years, to develop the pattern of being on the same radar screen. Being considerate of each other brings you even closer and makes for a solid and happy marriage.

The paper this morning contained an article about a lawsuit against a woman who had lost self-control and threw a hot cup of coffee in the face of someone who had aggravated her. It would appear that around 8 AM, in a busy station, a man somehow blocked the way of this woman and her cup of coffee. She cursed the man, who stopped to find out what he had done. Quickly, she threw the hot coffee in his face. He ended up in the hospital to be treated for burns. She was found guilty in court and was sentenced to pay a large fine for losing her temper. One cannot help but feel sorry for her husband, if she happens to be married.

Men also can lose control. In the same paper, another article featured a man who, a few days previous, had gotten on a bus already angry about the bus lines for some small mistake they had made. Without any warning, he started punching, of all people, a blind lady who could not defend herself. Fortunately several men came to her rescue and held the man until the police arrived.

Hear this: If an individual cannot control himself or herself while dating, believe me, he or she is not going to change when marriage has taken place. Self-control is needed—not only with one's temper, but also in finances, work, and recreation. It can be seen in these different areas when dating. Great is that individual who knows how to divide his time so that he gets his work completed without losing self-control.

One need only to look at the athletes in the Olympics to see the wisdom and value of controlling oneself. One area where self-control can be a serious problem is during a dispute, when voices are raised. Be careful not to call your spouse names or to make accusations that you know are not true. It is difficult to recall negative remarks.

Have you grown up emotionally? That is to say, have you accepted your gifts and liabilities and are you able to live with them and be content?

If you have, then this means that you can face problems and handle them without going into a deep depression. It means that you can develop relationships without compromising your convictions. It means that you can handle rejection and bounce back with enthusiasm. It means you can accept criticism and praise.

> **Conflict creates the fire of effects and emotions; and, like every fire, it has two aspects; that of burning and that of giving light.**
>
> **—Carl Jung**

Emotional maturity means that we can take care of ourselves. We are not seeking perfection in ourselves, but we seek to utilize our gifts. This is manifested in the way we love our spouse. We will go out of our way to meet the needs, aspirations, and desires of our spouse. We will not hesitate to put his or her needs ahead of our own.

Here is a case in point. An individual is in pharmacy research. He has a sharp intellect and can tell you what every pill in your medicine cabinet is able to do. He can give you the background of the pill industry and also a picture of things to come. Yet, on his honeymoon, he could not perform. This went on for several weeks, until his wife finally asked him what was wrong. It turned out that he was masturbating on a regular basis, as well as regularly looking at pornography. He was more interested in himself than in his wife. He was severely, emotionally immature.

> **If you don't like who you are and where you are, don't worry about it because you're not stuck either with who you are or where you are. You can grow. You can change. You can be more than who you are.**
>
> **—Zig Ziglar**

David Frisbel, in his book *Happily Remarried,* tells about Sheila:

> Sheila lives in the inner city. At age 38, she's a grandmother—twice. She has married twice and divorced twice. Her current male friend has been a part of her life

for nearly three years. She lives in his home. However, she is not seriously considering marrying him because he is too immature.

She goes on to say she might be willing to marry him someday, but not now. He has a lot of growing up to do.

Does emotional maturity mean that there will be no problems in the marriage? No. Wherever there are people, there will be problems. It does mean, however, that the two will be better able to manage their conflict, and it might in fact bring them even closer together.

Marriage affords the opportunity for one spouse to affirm the other spouse, and this should in turn strengthen their bond of love. A husband can do so much when he stands behind his wife and supports her. The same is true with the wife. One husband, who wanted to invite his boss and his boss's wife over for dinner, found his own wife was not willing to do this. But instead of condemning her, the husband suggested she call their pastor's wife, who does considerable entertaining. Furthermore, the husband went out of his way to reassure her and to assist wherever he could. When it was all over, the wife was most grateful to her husband for suggesting the dinner, which by the way, went very well.

In conclusion, it is almost impossible to have a happy and successful marriage without emotional maturity. I like the way Paul says it in 1 Corinthians 13:11:

> When I was a child, I spake as a child, I understood as a child, I thought as a child: but when I became a man, I put away childish things.

## Think About This!

Name three areas you would like to work on for yourself.

How will you do this?

# CHAPTER FOUR

## Where to Find a Spouse Worth Having

Contrary to popular thinking, there are untold numbers of singles waiting for the right individual to appear on the scene. How do I know this for sure? It is due to the fact that 50 percent of all adults over eighteen are single. This is an amazing reality when one is praying and hoping for a godly spouse. But, do I hear you asking, where are these choice, potential spouses?

Well, they are all around you. They live in your community, probably much closer than you realize!

As with most clergymen, it has been my practice to meet with a couple before their wedding day for marriage counseling. The standard for many churches is to have a minimum of three one-hour counseling sessions. Along with routine questions, we deal with how a couple met and the steps they took to break the ice and open up a conversation. The following illustrations suggest some of the possibilities available for those seeking a spouse worth having. One must keep in mind that these are not steps, but avenues that God has used to bring people together in marriage.

Without question, this is the number one place to find a spouse. That is obvious for a number of reasons. Here you probably will find a person with the same heartbeat as yours, the same Lord, the same faith, and the same interest in the things of God. Nothing is more wonderful than starting a new day sharing a devotional period with your spouse, recognizing that Jesus Christ is Lord.

> **The difficulty with marriage is that we fall in love with a personality, but we must live with a character.**
>
> **—Peter DeVries**

Several years ago, I was asked to organize some activities for older singles. This led to what we called "North of Forty." This group was to serve singles from forty to sixty years of age. Before long, there were seventy to eighty singles coming on a weekly basis. We had worship with contemporary music, followed by a Bible study or a guest speaker. Refreshments and a social time concluded the evening. It soon became apparent that the older group, those in their fifties and sixties, soon outnumbered those in their forties. This led to the formation of a group in their late thirties and forties. Ted Wallace, a forty-year old salesman for the Entertainment Book, and Gail Gommerman a thirty-nine-year old dental manager, accepted, independently of each other, the assignment of leading this group of forty year olds. Not only did they do a super job, but they also found in working together that their philosophy of leadership was similar. It was not long before they sensed that God was leading them into marriage. Their marriage has been a delight to watch, and the two sets of parents are so pleased.

> **The promises of God are the soul's compass, enabling us to chart our course even when the smothering fog of despair tempts us to doubt the goodness of the Father.**
>
> **—Richard Exley**

Many of us find it difficult to ask people to help us, but most people do not mind being called upon to assist in some activity or function.

Sally Peterson, a forty-five-year old salesperson, was very choosy when it came to accepting dates. She was a gifted harpist, and, as such, she purchased a most expensive instrument. It was heavy for Sally to lift into her station wagon, so she was dependent upon others to assist her. To make matters worse, she injured herself while on a cruise. As a result, she was helpless without assistance from others.

Active in our North of Forty group, Sally met Peter. He was a former missionary. When his marriage broke up, he returned to Toronto. His educational background led Peter to a new career in social work for children in the city. Sally needed assistance and found in Peter not only a source of help, but also eventually love! She leaned upon him to help her in the recovery of her health. She also was able to use Peter's vehicle to transport her harp to the venues where she was doing a recital. It was not long before Sally and Peter felt at home with one another. Actually, they each complemented the other. As they continued to work together, they grew closer and closer until Peter proposed marriage.

Yes, it all started when one needed help. The moral of the story is that one need not be hesitant to ask for assistance. As a matter of fact, most people like to be called upon to meet a particular need.

One year ago, I would never have recommended the Internet as a possible site for finding a spouse worth having. However, a few months ago this changed when Wilma Barrington spoke to me.

I was attending a seniors' function when Wilma came up to me with a broad smile and asked, "Do you remember me?" Well, there was no way we could forget her, as she had attended seniors' retreats and other sessions that I had organized. Wilma went on to say,

> Guess what? I have found a friend, and he is great. I am seventy-five, and he is seventy-five. His wife died seven years ago and my hubby ten years ago. We each have the same number of children, and we are both followers of Jesus Christ.

This led to the obvious question, "Where did you find Mr. Right?"

Her answer took me aback, and I was amazed when she said she had found him on the Internet. Actually, Wilma would be the last person to use the Internet. She is always so "proper" and conservative. She indicated that for some time she had been checking to view male prospects and that is how she came across Stan Gross. He met the criteria Wilma was looking for in a friendship. Likewise, she was all Stan could ever dream for in his hunt for a spouse. I said to her (in November 2008),

> "You will probably plan a wedding for next summer?"

> "Next summer! That's too far away. We want to go on a cruise before that!"

Wilma and Stan's wedding was on May 2, 2009, which was followed by the afore-mentioned cruise. Such is life!

**Second marriage is the triumph of hope over experience.**

**—Jim Smoke**

By the same token, I have seen a disaster!

Frank Jones's wife died from cancer. He started surfing the Internet and came upon two ladies from the same church. I am not sure if Frank knew that they were in the same church, but he made arrangements to see one of them, Dot Anderson, who was a divorcee. As he continued to look, he came upon Margaret, who seemed more interesting than Dot. Now, both Dot and Margaret were in the same singles group. You can imagine how Dot felt when Frank, who was going to see her, turned up with Margaret. We had some rough waters to smooth over.

Within a matter of two months, Margaret and Frank became engaged and started planning their wedding. Both were quite excited. They went to another church, which did not offer premarital guidance for their wedding.

About four years later, my telephone rang. It was Margaret Jones, who was crying. You can put the pieces together. Frank was not what she expected. His temper caused her to fear for her safety. In addition, he was using up her financial resources. And so the story went on and on. She wanted him out of the house. Eventually, they each hired a lawyer and I told them that at the rate they were going, they each would have to pay a fee of about $15,000 to $20,000. I recommended a negotiator, which they sought out, to help them with their final separation and divorce. Margaret and Frank were physically attracted to each other, but that was about all they had in common.

Chet and Dorothy Schneider knew Helen and Art Lewis when they were students at Wheaton College. As students, they participated in college functions, such as sports, drama, and concerts. During their working years, they had limited relationships. The Schneiders went as missionaries to Alaska. Art Lewis became a doctor in the Lancaster area of Pennsylvania. Over the years, the two couples kept in touch by way of Christmas cards and, on occasion, at alumni functions.

Art Lewis passed away, leaving Helen a widow at the age of seventy-four. Dorothy Schneider also died, leaving Chet a widower at the age of eighty-three. Helen, after hearing about Dorothy's death, sat down and wrote a special note of condolence to Chet. It was no ordinary letter, but one that really spoke to the heart and soul. She took time to share her own grief and was able to convey to Chet her deep expression of sympathy. She shared that life had never been the same and how different her life had become with the passing of Art.

Chet was so taken up with the note that he made contact with Helen. You know what is coming! Chet thought that if Helen felt that way, she would make a fine partner and helpmate in his later years of life. This led to Chet calling Helen to arrange for a visit. When they visited each other, it became very clear that their love and respect for each other was solid. And so they married, with the assurance that God had indeed brought them together.

**Four things come not back: the spoken word, the spent arrow, time past, the neglected opportunity.**
**—Ibn Al-Khattab Omar**

A library, a grocery store, a museum, and an art gallery are all fine places to meet a prospective spouse. One advantage to meeting at a library is the quietness of the room where one can carry on a conversation. Another advantage is that the two have a similar interest in reading and exploring the world.

The art gallery is another fine place to meet. Here two find a common interest and can share together their appreciation for art.

The grocery store is a natural place to meet, as we must all buy food. My brother Paul, after his divorce, was at the grocery store picking out items from the shelves when he met Sandy, an elementary school principal. Their eyes met and it was instant chemistry. It turned out that Sandy had just come through a divorce, like Paul, so they had much to talk about. They met again within a couple of days. They were soon taken up with each other and were married three months later. Well, there is no way one can get to know a future spouse well enough in such a short time. It did not surprise us that there were serious arguments and problems within weeks of their wedding. To make matters worse, Paul's two grown children did not get along with Sandy, nor did she enjoy their presence. This led to silence when they were together at the cottage. Paul was caught in the middle and did not see a way out, except for a breakup of the marriage.

> **Love and marriage may go together like a horse and carriage, but love and remarriage aren't as neatly complementary. The carriage may be so crowded that the horse has trouble pulling it.**
>
> **—Susan Kelly**

Have you noticed the increased number of older people returning to the classroom? Colleges and universities are offering more and more subjects of interest to older people. Classes on art, literature, history, psychology, and sociology are offered, many of them in the evening, making it possible for working people to enroll. One can readily see how you can meet another person with a similar interest if you are enrolled in the same study.

This provides a fine opportunity to meet for a meal before the evening class or a beverage after the session. You already have the topic to talk about, and perhaps you can help each other if there are assignments to be completed. In fact, the adults in this situation are likely more stable than most of those in other situations, because of their interests and willingness to do the assignments.

Dr. Jim Hughes, a Church of Christ minister in Dallas, Texas, told me about his ninety-one-year old mother, who had married another resident of her seniors' home, who was also ninety-one. Mrs. Hughes was a volunteer in the gift shop. She called Jim, her son, to say that a man was hanging around the shop. He was not a problem to her, but she soon discovered that he wanted to talk. So Jim encouraged his mother to be open but careful. Conversations soon followed between these two ninety-one-year old seniors. They started sitting together at meals and attended the evening entertainment together. Three months later, they were married. It was such a special affair that it made the television stations and the Dallas newspapers. They are very happy today and have a fine marriage.

> **You don't get to choose how you're going to die or when. You can only decide how you're going to live.**
> **—Joan Baez**

June Elliott, a sixty-five-year old divorcee, was leaving her room at the Sheppard Lodge in Toronto, when she met her new next-door neighbor, Lloyd Christie, an eighty-one-year old widower. They reached the parking lot, only to find that their parking spaces were next to each other. Well, you can appreciate how easy it would be to strike up a conversation, which they did immediately.

"Well, Lloyd, come and have dinner with me," June suggested. One dinner led to one lunch, and soon it became a habit to have meals together. They were married within six months.

Public transportation (streetcars, buses, airplanes, and trains) are fine places to meet a new person, because you are there for a set period of time until you reach your destination.

Now, I can speak from experience, because I met my wife on a streetcar, on my way to church. Actually, I was going to one church and she was going to another. Now I had seen her several years before, but did not know her name or anything about her. We got so involved in talking that I asked if we could sit together in church. It is hard to believe that sixty years later we still are sitting together. We celebrated our sixtieth wedding anniversary on December 27, 2008. God has been most gracious.

Cruises have brought many singles together. Here one must be careful, as a cruise is so different from ordinary living. On a cruise, everything is done for you! Passengers do not have to clean house, wash clothes, prepare meals, or shop. This means that it is not an easy task to really get to know an individual on a cruise, especially one you are thinking of marrying.

I asked my son, David, who is a lawyer, to address the North of Forty Singles and Single Again. He recently had come through a divorce, and so was single again. He spoke about legal matters affecting singles, such as the need to have a will and to have a power of attorney for health and finances. After the presentation, Elsie Jones, a divorcee, introduced herself. The two did not engage in conversation that evening. Three days later, David called and asked for Elsie Jones's phone number. It was my rule not to give out the phone numbers of our singles. However, I figured that Elsie had some legal questions and that David needed to contact her. He surprised us when, three weeks later, he called and asked if he could bring Elsie to our family quarterly birthday party. We discovered that they had been out on several dates and were actually getting serious about their relationship.

One year later, I officiated at their beautiful wedding. So, you never can tell how one brief greeting can lead to serious dating.

There are many magazines for singles and seniors that provide an address box, which can be used in developing a list of potential pen pals. This is a little like the Internet, and one must take the same precaution before giving your phone number and address. However, one advantage is that those who respond to your request most likely share your interests.

**My friends are my estate.**
**—Emily Dickinson**

What is nice about this approach is that you control the speed in the development of the relationship. There is no need to identify yourself until you are ready and you feel that the individual has qualities that attract you.

Over the years, people have cultivated some life-long friendships, yes, and even marriage. One must remember, however, that your pen pal may not be at all interested in marriage, but desiring a pal only for the interchange of ideas and interests.

It is possible that a parent, a sibling, a relative, or a friend may know of an individual who might be a good mate. It is wise to be open and not close the door on recommendations until you have had a chance to decide for yourself. This also can be applied to a blind date. Love is a fascinating thing, and you never can tell how it will strike you.

**Have courage for the great sorrows of life and patience for the small ones; and when you have laboriously accomplished your daily task, go to sleep in peace. God is awake.**

**—Victor Hugo**

Sheila Smith invited her girlfriend, Pamela Wilcox, to join her on a double date. Pamela did not know the fellows, but thought it would be fun. It turned out that Pamela's date was not as interesting or as attractive as Paul Henderson, the fellow who went with Sheila. You guessed it—Paul called Pamela the next week and suggested a date. Chemistry was good and one year later they were married.

This is a natural way to meet folks. With dog walking, you have similar interests and you can always talk about your dogs. Furthermore, it is a daily task that must be done morning and evening. In addition, you are walking the same streets and parks, twice a day. You can see how easy it is to meet others. You have instant conversation and perhaps look out for one another, from time to time.

> **I've been on so many blind dates I should get a free dog.**
>
> **—Wendy Leibman**

Esther Thompson has taken on the task of walking dogs in her community. She serves about eight families and will even take on caring for the dogs while the owners are on vacation. It is amazing what she learns about people, their habits, their way of living, their homes, and their work. She discovers, to some degree, the way the husband and wife are getting along, and she is aware of those experiencing domestic problems and of others who might be ready to dissolve their marriage.

More than one husband has shown an interest in Esther, who always dresses well and looks sharp. Due to the recent death of her husband, she has not responded or encouraged her possible suitors. It is because of Esther's husband's recent death that she is not interested. But it shows the potential.

In these tough economic times, the need for food banks and clothing depots increases. They depend upon volunteers to man them. This involves receiving the goods, sorting them, and then distributing them. This is a good way to find people who tend to be generous and helpful. Such characteristics in people are great to form both temporary and permanent relationships.

Although I do not personally know people who have been working in this area and found their lifelong spouse, I can see where this would be a super ministry in which to be engaged.

Try working with a rescue mission. Here you provide a meal for many who are homeless. You arrive early to assist the permanent staff with cooking, setting tables, and preparing food baskets. I know of two different couples, who as singles assisted with a downtown rescue mission and later married.

It may well be that you are shy and tend to keep to yourself. Perhaps you have low self-esteem. Feeling inferior can keep you to yourself. If you are ever going to meet others, you must get out where others are working, playing, or reading.

**It is not a lack of love, but a lack of friendship that makes unhappy marriages.**
**—Friedrich Nietzsche**

Social events such as line dancing, bowling, golfing, and other activities present opportunities where you can meet other folks interested in the things that hold your interest. Every Saturday, throughout the warm summer months, the singles of The North of Forty Singles and Single Again meet to play miniature golf. They choose a course that presents a great challenge and that leads to fine discussion and interchange. A social time with refreshments takes the group to the noon hour.

Over the course of time, a number of relationships have developed between members of the group.

Not only is this good for your health, but it also opens up the possibility for meeting Mr. or Ms. Right. Here you have a common goal—a strong and healthy body, and common interests—the tools for keeping one in shape. It is also a very natural place to carry on a conversation, with topics that are of interest to everyone. Here you talk about weights and the various techniques and tools that are available.

Our son ran a fitness club, and it was interesting to see the different ages of people and their marriage status. It was so easy to strike up a conversation with the people while they were going through their programs.

> **If you think you can, you can, and if you think you can't, you're right.**
>
> **—Mary Kay Ash**

It is not difficult to imagine how easy it might be to meet a potential future spouse in a fitness club.

Our political parties welcome volunteers to make telephone calls, take down signs, fold letters, stuff envelopes, and do a million other jobs.

**We waste time looking for the perfect lover, instead of creating the perfect love.**

**—Tom Robbins**

The kinds of people who volunteer for this are usually outgoing and have a fairly positive outlook on life. Would you agree that they are good prospects for friendships? And this is where permanent relationships are formed, beginning with a fine relationship. The conversation naturally comes around to talking about the one running for office, both his principles and philosophy of life. As issues are raised, you include them in your conversation.

You can readily see how life-long relationships can be formed among those participating in a choral group. Some take off and travel to Europe as a singing group. Many times you have a social period together, which opens the way for developing friendships that later lead to marriage.

> **Though I am always in haste, I am never in a hurry; because I never undertake any more work than I can go through with perfect calmness of spirit.**
> **—John Wesley**

Melody Latirilla was going with an older gentleman when she met a fellow Filipino, Elbern Catanus, in a choral group. She became friends with Elbern, and two years later they were married.

Here one can be a participant by actually joining a team or by becoming a coach of a little league for boys and girls. In these situations, you meet single parents, who come to watch their kids play. Again, there are opportunities for meeting parents and developing positive relationships.

Karen Peterson had a child out of wedlock with a previously married professional, who was not prepared to marry her at that time. When her daughter started playing soccer at the age of eight, Karen took an active interest. The following year they needed a coach, and she volunteered and had a great time. It filled her long summer evenings and afforded her daughter an opportunity to be active in sports.

There are singles' groups in most cities. You will find that the ladies outnumber the men, about four to one. However, it is an open door to meet folks, especially single men, who are, for the most part, ready for friendship.

Singles' clubs carry on many various activities—socials, cruises, volunteer work, and sports.

## 20—Join a Service Club

Various service groups like the Rotary Club, the Lyons, and a host of others meet in the city on a regular basis. Many take on projects. The Rotary Club in the City of Guelph sponsored a solution to the water problem in Peru.

This is a fine way to meet people with the same interests and a desire to help society at large. They conduct dinners, to which others are invited, and you have the opportunity to meet and develop new relationships.

Wrapping up this chapter, one must not overlook their appearance and the impression we present to others. It is not a matter of wearing $500 suits or $300 dresses. Are our clothes somewhat in style, and are they clean and neat? Does our hair look like we just got out of bed? Take a look at your shoes and overall appearance. Would you like to know someone who dresses and looks like you?

Some years ago, a lady in her mid-twenties came up to me after the morning service and said: "I am disappointed with God!"

"Well," I asked, "why?"

She said, "Look at me. Here I am twenty-six years old and I still do not have a husband."

She was blaming God, and yet she did not sense that maybe her personal appearance was her problem. Her hair was a mess, her clothes were soiled, and there was no reason for this, as she had a position that brought her a steady income. It was simply her way of living. Looking back, I should have confronted her about her appearance and sent her to my wife for guidance. She was quite critical of others, and it would appear to me that she had low self-esteem. She conveyed the Turkish proverb: *Who seeks a faultless friend remains friendless.*

One way to develop self-esteem is to cultivate friends. With friends around you, you smile more and feel better. This actually gives you energy. You treat people better. You become a better person.

**Change your thoughts and you change your world.**
**—Norman Vincent Peale**

This is where our faith can make a big difference. Seeking to honor our Lord leads us to love people and to be able to minister to them. This changes our appearance. We smile more and people will smile back at us.

## Wrap Up

The material in this chapter can change your life if you will take time to study the suggestions. Yes, this will require discipline and probably a change in your schedule. Start with what will be easy and progress from there.

## Think About This

Choose two things you have not tried and apply them within a week.

1. ................................................................................................................

   ................................................................................................................

   ................................................................................................................


2. ................................................................................................................

   ................................................................................................................

   ................................................................................................................

# CHAPTER FIVE

## Have You Met These Couples?

You can benefit from others who have had a very successful marriage. It has been a delight to interview over thirty couples, who, in my judgment, appear to have a happy marriage. All have been married from five to fifty years or more. This was the question they were asked to respond to:

> Apart from the spiritual, share with me at least three things that have made your marriage such a success.

Now, you will find in their answers many similar traits, even though they did not discuss the question with others. It is suggested that you choose three of the traits that you consider useful for your situation. Note that most names have been changed, but not always their occupation. Also note that each testimony represents a couple that I know personally. In other words, no response was made up.

*Ted Johnson is a retired worship leader and his wife served with him in an active role at the church.*

Thank you for asking us. We enjoyed talking about what has made our marriage successful (and had some fun doing it) and, after almost forty-seven years of marriage, trying to put our thoughts and feelings into words has been great.

This is what we came up with. It may not be the qualities that others are looking for, but this is our list (the items listed are not necessarily in order of importance):

1.  One whose love is evident—love for God and love for their spouse
2.  One who is kind and seeks to do what is good for their spouse and for others. I have been reading the book of Titus for my devotions, and four times in this short letter, Paul tells Titus to stress to the people that they should give themselves to "doing what is good."
3.  One who is warm and has a gentle personality as opposed to being uncompromising and insistent.

We also considered qualities such as "being my best friend," "caring," "loyal," "trustworthy," and "having a sense of humor" as being important.

> **Marriage is that relationship between man and woman in which the independence is equal, the dependence mutual, and the obligation is reciprocal.**
> **—Louis K. Anpacher**

*Joe Turpin was a printer for many years and his wife was a stay-at-home mom.*

Our marriage vows have been very meaningful to us. We have tried to love, honor, and obey throughout our marriage. To us, without trust you have nothing, and so it has been the primary focus in our marriage. Divorce has never been an option except in the event of infidelity. We have found that you have to work through "for richer, for poorer, for better, for worse." Always try, if you have had an argument, to resolve it before going to bed.

> **Remember, we all stumble, every one of us. That's why it's a comfort to go hand in hand.**
> **—Emily Kimbrough**

*Ryan Sikakane was a seminary professor and his wife, Minnie, a stay-at-home mom.*

I am not sure that I can speak to "what makes a successful marriage." It is not as if we sat down and mapped things out systematically as to what we were going to do, and how and when. It has been all of God's grace; I cannot even say we are "super-spiritual," because we are not. There are some factors that have come into play.

In our culture, marriage is understood to be a lifetime commitment. Amazulu do not practise what are called arranged marriages as they do in India. Commitment is taught by example. Married people live together all of their married lives. That is what young people growing up come to understand. And there are procedures in place to deal effectively with situations that might lead to separation. Marriage is a serious arrangement between two families, which responsible young people will not easily flout. The bride-to-be is confined to her room with several experienced ladies who counsel her intensively. Their words are indelibly etched on the young girl's heart and mind. The elderly people's experience is always highly respected. However, some of these practices have fallen by the wayside as western ways have taken over.

Minnie and I met at a teacher training college. We heard and accepted the gospel. We understood what it meant to be followers of Jesus Christ properly, but not fully. God protected us by His grace. Upon graduation, both of us were recommended to teach in different schools of the same mission. I started teaching before Minnie completed her training because she was my junior. As I shared the gospel with our students, a mini revival began and spilled over to surrounding schools. There was a great group of committed young people, both in my school and in the one where Minnie began teaching.

Fellowship with them greatly strengthened our faith. In fact, Minnie was baptized by immersion at the school where she taught before we were married. A year and a half after we got married, when our firstborn was just a baby, I felt the call to go to Bible school. That was when our married life began in earnest. Big decisions had to be made. Minnie displayed courage and faith I never thought she had. Even though she was not unsure about me leaving teaching and going to Bible school, once she was convinced that I should, she never looked back. When I resigned from Bible school because our second child was on the way, and Minnie had to stop teaching, she would not accept that. She told me that the Lord is able to support widows, and that is what happened.

When I joined the teaching staff at Bible school, our salary was fifteen pounds to live on and to support our five children. We depended on honoraria during vacation, when I went around preaching and teaching. Minnie just fasted and prayed, prayed, prayed. We both took our calling seriously. We were committed to what we had to do. Money was not an issue. We faced lots of health problems with our young family. We prayed for them and with them in our daily family altar. We got lots of encouragement from people like the principal of the Bible college, who wanted to see me replace him as principal. Michael Cassidy was sure that I could have a significant ministry within African Enterprise. I ended up ministering in thirty countries around the world. We found many such affirmations from our colleagues.

We have had disagreements and arguments as a couple at home and they ended as that. We did not allow these to happen in the presence of our children. Nor did they ever become a shouting match with raised voices. We settled the problem between ourselves with the Lord's help. Here again, as we compared notes, our parents, who in many ways were similar, were good models for us to follow.

> **Be not angry that you cannot make others as you wish them to be, since you cannot make yourself as you wish to be.**
>
> **—Thomas à Kempis**

*Nathan and Pam are retired schoolteachers. They celebrated their fortieth year of marriage in 2009. This is their story.*

On May 31, 2009, we celebrated forty years of marriage. Most of them have been absolutely fabulous, but a few of them have been challenging.

The one thing that brought us through these shaky years was just pure commitment. On our wedding day, we promised each other that only death would separate us. When it seemed like our love for each other was very low and almost non-existent, we hung in there and knew that we would continue to be husband and wife, regardless of our feelings. And because we honored our wedding vows, our love for one another always has returned, and returned stronger than ever. Every marriage goes through rough times, but if you persevere and try to make it work, your love for each other will come back.

**Love works wonders.**
**—Marguerite de Navarre**

We also learned early in our marriage that it is so important to respect each other. Whether alone or with friends, we have never belittled or made fun of the other person or put them down. We have respected each other's gifts, talents, and uniqueness and realized that together we are more than the sum total of just two. We have had our fights and disagreements, but in the middle of the battle, we have tried never to say anything hurtful or degrading. We have realized that whatever comes out of our mouths can never be taken back. Our words can lift up or tear down because our tongues are very powerful.

When life became very busy with children, careers and the cares of life, we always tried to spend time together. After each evening meal and before the dishes were done, we would take our coffee into the living room and get caught up on the day's events. We shared a few moments together. The children knew that this was our time. We made an effort to continue going out on dates, and when possible, to get away for a couple of days to renew our love for one another. And now that the children are grown and we are once again alone, we continue to be each other's best friend, because we valued our relationship above all else. We have learned that when mom and dad love and respect each other, the children feel secure and loved.

We have discovered that life and marriage can be very challenging. But with commitment and respect for each other, and spending quality time together, marriage will blossom and grow.

> **To keep your marriage brimming with love in the loving cup, whenever you're wrong, admit it; whenever you're right, shut up.**
>
> **—Ogden Nash**

*Jack Smith worked in the shipping department of a large book publisher, and Gail was a secretary before she became a stay-at-home mom.*

Jack let Gail do most of the talking as to what has made their marriage a success. However, he did say that he believed the major reason his marriage was so great had to do with choosing the right mate. Spouses can differ so much, but you should be sure that the one you marry is compatible with your temperament and style.

Gail says that for her part, it has been all about taking good care of Jack's needs. Throughout their fifty-five years of marriage, she has tried to anticipate his needs and meet them.

> **One of the greatest forms of respect we can extend to another is friendship. Friendship accepts other people for who they are and stands by them in difficult moments.**
>
> **—Stephen R. Covey**

*Nathan and his wife, Lorna, are realtors and developers of residences for seniors.*

Many years ago, we committed our marriage to the Lord. We believe that the Lord was our matchmaker and He brought us together. As such, He is the foundation of our marriage. We have been able to love and respect each other as we acknowledge the presence of Jesus Christ in our home. He is the one who has given us the strength to stay together, in spite of the bumps we have had along the way.

*Bob Danielson was an executive with Bell and he and his wife will soon be celebrating their sixtieth wedding anniversary.*

Here are some of the reasons for our successful marriage. During the first year of our marriage, some sixty years ago, my wife Sue and I committed our lives to our Lord Jesus Christ. This act of commitment to follow Jesus has provided us with strength and guidance throughout our life together. Made us perfect? No! Taught us the meaning and value of humbling ourselves before God and man? Yes!

Early in our journey of faith, we began to realize that God seldom does what He can do until we do what we must do. For instance, "Trust in the Lord with all your heart, and lean not on your own understanding. In all your ways acknowledge Him, and He will direct your paths" (Prov. 3:5, 6).

My wife and I have always shown each other a high degree of respect and trust. We never take one another for granted. We have found that good communication within our marriage works well in promoting the respect and trust that we expect from each other.

In our marriage we discovered that a major key to a successful relationship is to be good financial managers. This involves strong discipline, especially in our materialistic society where marketing people urge us to spend dollars that we do not always have. In our view, poor management of personal finances can and does fracture relationships.

We realize that it takes a lot of hard work from both parties in a marriage for it to be successful. Nothing is for free. But our God has richly blessed us and we praise His name continually.

**The quality of your life is the quality of your relationships.**

**—Anthony Robbins**

*Steve Kenny has been a professional football player and his wife, Sherry, is a social worker.*

Looking back on our thirty-plus years of marriage, three things stand out in our minds.

1.  We have had shared core values. Our dreams and our hopes have flowed from our shared values.
2.  We have recognized and accepted our individual strengths and weaknesses. We share a mutual respect for our differences.
3.  We have a passionate, unconditional love for one another and for God.

This is foundational if any marriage is to succeed.

*Keith Buehler has been a pastor for over forty years, and his second wife, Katharine, formerly worked in Hollywood, California, as an actress.*

Keith and Katharine both have been divorced. As they planned their marriage, three things came to mind:

1. Our first marriages were not marked by openness and honor.
2. In our marriage, we are going to have a positive attitude toward each other. We do not want to make negative remarks about one another as we did in our first marriages.
3. We are very content with our present situation and intend to remain content with our present situation and home.

*Here is a tribute by a truck and ambulance driver and his wife. She was a schoolteacher, who after the children had grown up, went back to teaching.*

Our relationship has been based on respect and trust from the early days. After forty-five years of the ups and downs of life, that respect and trust remains, plus a deeper love than ever!

Calling to let the other know of delays or changes in plans, not making major purchases without consulting each other, not opening each other's mail or going into each other's wallet or purse without permission have been evidences of mutual respect. However, once because we were running late, my husband packed my suitcase for our trip. It never happened again! He was and still is very helpful with household tasks. We were in the midst of a move and he efficiently packed as I looked after food and the children. As we were about to leave, we couldn't find the baby's diapers. They were packed, somewhere. Because I was able to be a full-time homemaker, we shared the responsibility for family meals, homework, paper routes, and taking the children to sports and music activities.

We have not always agreed with each other, but try to settle differences before going to bed. Sometimes bedtime has been quite delayed! A sense of humor has often saved the day.

We have enjoyed many adventures with our children, including having student boarders and some international guests in our home, travels to Prince Edward Island, British Columbia, Alabama, and Florida. Our lives have been enriched by people from all backgrounds and walks of life. Moving several times created the opportunity to make new friends. We holiday together and value times spent with our grandchildren. Time spent visiting shut-ins gives us a lift as we admire their acceptance of their limitations. We do gardening and walk together as we strive to maintain our health. Individually, we spend some time with friends of the same sex.

Very important to the longevity of our marriage is the fact that we left our parents (but did not abandon them) and have been firmly loyal to each other as best friends. Life-threatening illnesses have strengthened our bond. As someone has said, "We treasure most that which we have lost."

Anyone who has been blessed with true friendship knows the cost and the worth.

—M. Basie Pennington

*Allan Calvert, when asked about his marriage, wrote some poetry in a tribute to his wife. One can see in his lines the precious traits of his wife, Norma.*

You come as a garden of flowers
The breath of the light of the sun
The rise of the reaching of towers
The laughter of rivers that run
The fragrance of dawning of morning
The whisper of Aeolian sound
The warmth of a season of summer
The joy of a new day begun.
You fall on my soul as a raindrop
As fresh as the fanfare of rain;
You fill my cup with sweetness
And pour to its fullness again.
How oft in your smile, as a token
Exposing the depth that you are
I am turned as a creature of gladness
To places that reach to afar.
Where tomorrow rides swift in the pathway
Where memories fill their display
And fashion rich treasure for keeping
To spur times exquisite replay.

**Love is the condition in which the happiness of another person is essential to your own.**

**—R.A. Heinlein**

*A dentist, Dr. Stan Clappison, reflected back on nearly sixty years of marriage.*

Being happily married for nearly sixty years makes a couple exceptional and unusual. Many in modern society have lost the meaning of commitment. Even in evangelical churches, the influence of movies, television, and books have cheapened marriage, changed the meaning of love to lust, and made sex almost like a spectator sport! So when folks learn of our enduring marriage, they inevitably ask, or think, "How did you do it?"

Speaking for myself, I can only say that I have learned as I have gone along. I did not have a great example to follow, as my parents did not have a very happy marriage and there was not a lot of love shown from day to day. I did not realize this when I was growing up, but now as an adult I look back with the clarity that comes from hindsight.

Marriage is a learning experience for all couples. When the sexual attraction that brings them together wears off, they begin to discover habits and quirks in each other that they never saw before. Then they begin a lifelong journey of getting used to each other's faults and also of discovering some of the failings as well as some of the great resources of character and love each of us brings to a marriage.

My wife has been and still is a wonderful loving partner and a great supporter of my entrepreneurial spirit and business ideas. Without her, I could not have achieved many of the goals I had for my business and professional life. She learned a great deal about marriage from the example set by her parents, who surmounted enormous difficulties caused by a very serious accident. She has great people skills and radiates beauty of personality to all who know her.

We have had many problems to overcome in our married life. Since both of us are only children and come from different countries, our Christian faith has been a real help to us, and we have sought to live it out before our children and their families.

We thank the Lord that we are still blessed with good health and able to enjoy our lives together, trusting and loving each other without reservation.

A successful marriage requires falling in love many times, always with the same person.

—**Mignon McLaughlin**

*Read the testimony of Dr. James Wallace, who has served churches in the United States and Canada.*

What makes a lasting marriage? My wife and I have been happily married for almost fifty years. What is our secret? Well, we got off to a good start.

**A vigorous five mile walk will do more good for an unhappy but otherwise healthy adult than all the medicine and psychology in the world.**
**—Paul Dudley White**

We were believers and became acquainted with each other while both of us were involved in the ministry of Stouffville Youthtime. Since our wedding, this partnership has continued across the years.

Early in our marriage, we learned that men and women think and act differently and that this is by God's design. This meant that we had a three-dimensional perspective on life and on any issues we might face. Remembering this has led us to request each other's insight on whatever situation we were confronting. It has been easy for us to discuss how any particular situation should be handled and to review the results afterwards to determine if a better approach could be taken in the future. This has helped us to avoid making impetuous decisions that would have been detrimental. At the same time, it has been a mutual appreciation for each other's support.

Over the years in ministry, we have observed that for many couples their major difficulties have involved unresolved offences and unfilled expectations. This is where freedom of communication is so important. Instead of nursing hurts and disappointments that tend to fog up the atmosphere and put a negative connotation on other situations, and knowing that our relationship was couched in love, it has been liberating to express our concerns, resolve them, and go on happily enjoying each other.

In the case of disagreement or offense, we recognized early in our marriage that the silent treatment did not work. It was much better to talk things out, while appreciating each other's position. So we agreed to express ourselves without delay and without recrimination, with a willingness to say, "I'm sorry!" and "Thank you for your counsel!" We have found that in this kind of loving relationship, we could handle any type of problem and work it out amicably.

> **You cannot change what happened in the past, neither can I. What you can change is what you can do in the future.**
>
> **—Unknown**

I am also pleased to say that across the years we have been aware of each other's basic need, security for my wife and affirmation for myself. So far as I am aware, I have not given any reason for my wife to be suspicious that I might have a romantic interest in any other woman. And, gratefully, my wife has always been ready to encourage me by affirming wise decisions and proper action.

Every marriage is presumably the result of the couple being in love with each other. If this is so, why do so many fail? For a marriage to be a good and lasting one, the couple must have a proper understanding of what true love really is. We use the term "love" rather loosely, speaking of the kinds of food we love, things we love to do, and even the television programs we love to watch. But what is real love? What is the kind of love that makes a marriage work? It is not that "I love what you do for me" or "I love how you make me feel" or "I love how you look." In light of the sacrificial love Christ Jesus has demonstrated for us, we have understood that true love means before I think of myself, I desire the other's security, happiness, and contentment. This is my primary responsibility. Practicing this kind of love and support for each other, our relationship has continued strong and growing across these many years.

Add to these delights the blessing of family and friends, and we can only say with gratitude to God, "Thank you, Lord!" for these wonderful years.

> **Lord, when we are wrong, make us willing to change, and when we are right, make us easy to live with.**
>
> **—Peter Marshall**

*Andrew Kim tells how he met his wife, Joy, and the great marriage they have been enjoying for many years.*

Joy and I met when I moved to Montreal to do my master of social work degree at McGill University. A medical student from Newfoundland and I went out Sunday nights to different churches. Then one night, we worshipped at Westmount Baptist Church.

After the service, a friendly young man asked if we were new to the church and to the city. He then proceeded to invite us to participate in their youth group on Friday night. Joy was a sixteen-year old teenager at the time, and she was part of the youth group. We got to know each other well, but it was not until seven years later that we started dating.

> **Except Thou build it, Father,**
> **The house I build is in vain:**
> **Except Thou, Savior, bless**
> **My joy will turn to pain:**
> **But nought can break,**
> **Our hearts in Thee are one**
> **And love Thy Spirit hallows**
> **Is endless love.**
>
> **—John Ilerton**

On October 24th, we will be celebrating our thirty-ninth anniversary. I thank God for seeing us through some unexpected and unsuspected storms of life, which have included major surgeries for Joy and a career change on my part. I went from a professional social worker and social planner to that of being a minister.

If I were to reflect on our blessed marriage, I attribute it to God in bringing us together. The most important reason for the "success" of our marriage is that we share the same values, especially those of social justice, concern for the disadvantaged, and our fidelity to and faith in Jesus Christ. Values are what you and I hold as true and dear. These are not just empty words, because we are to be guided by them in our everyday behavior and conduct and in how we make our decisions, both large and small.

Joy is a terrific loving mother and now grandmother. She still remembers the temperatures our children had when they were young. She puts our children first and foremost and above her own interests every day.

Joy is not at all materialistic, as her family did not have much money while she was growing up. Her minister-turned-doctor father died an untimely death, leaving her mother to bring up two small children. To this day, she never aspires to have fancy apparel or expensive jewelry. We never quarrel about money, as we always try to live within our means. We give away to good causes as much as we can. Until she retired a year ago, Joy worked in neurophysiology in hospitals and loved her patients by going out of her way to help them.

Joy is an extrovert, making friends easily with people of all different backgrounds; she likes people and accepts everyone quite readily. She makes a point of making friends with those who are divorced or widowed, as many would otherwise lead a rather lonely life.

Joy is a good forgiver, as we do not carry grudges over long periods of time. This does not mean that she does not have a temper, but it rarely is displayed.

I love Joy for all of the above qualities, along with her love for reading and travel, which we both enjoy. And most of all, I thank God for her generous spirit in persevering with me over the years.

What Andrew says about his wife, for the most part, is seen in his life as well!

> **I would like to engraved inside every wedding band: "Be kind to one another." This is the golden rule of marriage and the secret of making love last through the years.**
>
> **—Randoloh Ray**

*A high school art teacher tells of his happy marriage to his wife of over forty years.*

My wife, Dorothy, and I grew up in Hamilton, Ontario. We were both from working class families. We attended different high schools, and didn't meet until we both had become teachers and were attending extension classes at McMaster University. We met regularly at the bus stop on the way to classes and got a ride home with another classmate. Our friendship blossomed and eventually we were married. We shared a house with my parents (not an ideal situation, since my mother's health was very poor), and after my dad died, my mother became very dependent on us.

Dorothy and I shared the same hobby, and we began to develop the habit of planning our lives with consideration for each other's needs and schedules. We only had one car, and so transportation issues required a lot of give-and-take, especially when I got a job in another city and commuted for a year. Since we were never blessed with children of our own, we were able to travel (usually to special events connected with our hobby) and spend much time together, comfortable in each other's presence and not always having to fill up any silence with talking or extraneous noise.

**And they lived happily ever after is one of the most tragic sentences in literature. It's tragic because it is a falsehood. It is a myth that has led generations to expect something from marriage that is not possible.**
**—Joshua Licyman**

Our interests were similar, but for many years they didn't involve spiritual matters. When my wife encountered a potentially serious illness, I turned to the Lord for strength to deal with it and accepted Christ as my Savior. My wife had become a Christian as a teenager, but had moved away from Him until this later period of life. We began to attend church and became very involved with ushering, Sunday School teaching, and other ministries in the church. When for a period of seven months I was out of work, we drew very close to the Lord and to each other.

This was an important period of spiritual growth for both of us. We have accepted invitations to serve in leadership roles in the church (elder, deacon, lay pastor, committee member, and chairperson) and have grown with each challenge and responsibility.

We both have learned in fifty-three years of marriage to put the Lord first, our partner second, and ourselves third. We have learned to be faithful in stewardship, to avoid debt (we have rarely had to pay any credit interest), and to respond to the needs of others around us.

*Now we have a school administrator share his views on marriage after forty years of living with a schoolteacher, his wife.*

To build a successful marriage relationship, a couple must be willing to work on developing a true friendship. My wife and I, as individuals, are distinctly different in our likes and dislikes. I'm a sports enthusiast; she's not. I like TV documentaries; she likes murder mysteries. I am a loner; she likes company. I am not a talker; she's very much a conversationalist. An analysis, from my perspective, would lead one to conclude that our marriage would be fraught with misunderstanding and conflict. Not so! Though we experienced a fair amount of turbulence in the first couple of years of our marriage, we have enjoyed a peaceful and mutually fulfilling relationship.

> **The more connections you and your lover make, not just between your bodies, but between your minds, your hearts, and your souls, the more you will strengthen the fabric of your relationships, and the more real moments you will experience together.**
> **—Barbara De Angelis**

Much of the success of our relationship can be attributed to the fact that, in spite of our personality differences, we have cultivated a strong friendship. The bedrock of that friendship has been the high regard we have given to our marriage vows. On our wedding day, we made a lifelong commitment to each other. In our vows we stated the words "till death do us part," and we meant it. The door was locked and the key thrown away! So on the basis of that understanding—that we are primarily committed to each other, no matter what—we have become the best of friends.

Having such a diverse set of likes and dislikes, it has taken some effort to develop true friendship. It was not automatic. Both of us have had to be willing to show compromise in our areas of interest and personal preference. For example, Brenda has zero interest in major league baseball. I, on the other hand, quite enjoy baseball and will attend a game whenever the opportunity arises. Yet, I never go alone. Brenda is usually with me. She'll sit through nine full innings, paying attention only when the home team hits a home run. Instead of trying to follow a game, which holds no interest for her, she will bring along a good book, so it becomes a positive experience for both of us. The important fact is that we are together.

> **We have two ears and one mouth so we can listen twice as much as we speak.**
>
> **—Epictetus**

Then there are times when Brenda wants to attend a new box office release that interests her. It may not be a story line that appeals to me at all. However, I will go along, and we will enjoy an evening at the movies. Interestingly enough, more and more I'm finding that I quite enjoy the movie she chooses. Whether I do or not, however, is not important. The important thing is that we're together. Brenda is my best friend and I want to be with her.

As our lives have become intertwined through "doing life together" and through giving priority to building a strong friendship, there has developed an unbreakable trust between us. I have come to know my wife intimately as an individual and can trust her implicitly. She, in turn, places that same level in me. Our only secrets are the ones we mutually share.

As we have majored on developing a deep and trusting friendship, we have been able to deal with the many curves that life throws our way with the strength of two—not just one. The payoff, in terms of peace in the home and security for the entire family, has been immeasurable.

*The captain of a fire station, located in the downtown area of a large city, the third busiest station in North America, does not exactly have a lot of time on his hands, but read his response to marriage.*

I suppose for each one of us when we reach important milestones in our lives we ask the question, "Where did the time go—it seems like only yesterday." We were married in St. Barnabas Church on September 19, 1959. We built our relationship, not with the expectation of always being perfect, but on love, trust, and the many blessings God has given to us. On the day we said our vows, I don't think we realized that marriage is hard work. It's not only about being with the one you have chosen and love, but being with that person everyday, sharing ideas and dreams "till death us do part."

**Aim for success, not perfecton. Never give up your right to be wrong, because you will lose the ability to learn new things and move forward with your life.**
**—Dr. David M. Burnas**

During the years, we have always tried to treat each other with respect and caring. My husband is my rock. He can settle me down when I overreact and become anxious. We raised three children, and although the times were simpler then, when a problem arose we would talk about it and try to solve it together. We have wonderful memories of those growing-up years with our children and wouldn't trade them for the world.

We tried to put spaces in our togetherness and to pursue our own interests. These times apart were special to each one, and they strengthened our ties as a couple. Fortunately, we both have a sense of humor, and at times that's what gets us through; we can't imagine not sharing laughter. Through the years, the involvement with our families has always been important to us, and those good times together always are filled with fun and laughter.

When we first moved into our home forty-six years ago, we found our place of worship at St. Jude's. We were young with children and became involved immediately. That was our fortunate day, and the friends we met there became our other family. The friendships that we made during those years have been filled with the happiness of birth and the sorrows of death. We have shared the "ups" and "downs" of raising our families and enjoyed parties and holidays together. Our worship at this place has been very important to us and has given us a special understanding and love of life.

Fifty years . . . when we reflect back we can't believe it, but here we are still sharing each new day that God gives us and enjoying every moment.

At our fiftieth wedding anniversary, the pastor who gave the prayer for the meal said before praying that he has given all husbands the secret of a long and lasting marriage. I wondered what he was going to say. Let me put it in his own words:

> As we celebrate with George this happy day, he has taught us who are husbands the secret of a long marriage. It is always falling in love, again and again, but always with the same lady, your wife.

*Robin Smith gives the following response to the question, What kept your marriage together? He and his wife, Ethel, took seriously the words of the wedding ceremony, "Till death do us part." It was a promise made to each other and now after fifty years, it is being kept and they are enjoying their days together.*

Robin and Ethel believe in communication and have never applied the silent treatment. Over the years, they have talked things over, both the big and the small. They confess that over the years it has taken work by both of them to have a successful marriage. They recognized the importance of telling each other, "I love you and you are important to me."

Mind you, a good sense of humor can help in your relationship with each other. They said they still can laugh at themselves. This started when they first married and has continued to this day.

> **Humor is affirmation of dignity, a declaration of man's superiority to all that befalls him.**
>
> **—Romain Gary**

*Herb and Georgina Ford have been married—to each other—for over fifty-seven years! People are amazed, even incredulous, when they learn that the couple has been married for over half a century. In this day and age of a forty-five percent divorce rate among those who have been married for the first time, the longevity of the Fords' marriage begs the question, how have they done it?*

The answer is simple: most importantly, by the grace of God, and also in being faithful to one another.

Theirs has been a labor of love. Through thick and thin, the good times and the not-so-good, the easy and the difficult, they have honored the vows that they made to one another long ago. As a result, their marriage has stood the test of time.

Herb and Georgina have served the Lord together gladly all these years, have raised a family where all their children and grandchildren have put their faith in the Lord Jesus Christ, and have trusted Him to help them face all the challenges that have come their way.

The apostle Paul wrote to the Corinthian believers that those who marry will have many troubles in this life (1 Cor. 7:28), and the Fords have been no exception. But they would testify that, through it all, the Lord has kept, helped, and blessed them abundantly.

*In closing this chapter, notice the tribute Vance Havner gives to his wife in his book* Peace in the Valley. *(118)*

I had often wondered how it would be if sickness befell me. Well, the day has come, and my better half has been as wonderful in sickness as in health. It is not good for man to dwell alone, and to be sick alone is disastrous. I rejoice in a partnership that stands the test. I thank God increasingly for a life companion who is just sweet and faithful. Her sweetness is expressed in deed and faithfulness.

> **She is a winsome wee thing,**
> **She is a handsome wee thing,**
> **She is lo'esome wee thing,**
> **This sweet wee wife of mine.**
> **—Bobbie Burns**

The years have built up a wealth of tender memories that speak of a wife's constant care. When Sara travels with me, I look for her in the congregation first thing, and she still laughs at my humor as though she were hearing it for the first time. The many gentle suggestions that have smoothed rough corners and improved my preaching, the scores of nuisances she has shielded me from, in order to make my load lighter—for all of this, no amount of words in cold type can say enough. When the rewards are handed out, I am sure that not all the medals will go to those who went forth to battle. There will be many a crown for wives who tarried by the stuff.

> **Love is the ability and willingness to allow those that**
> **you care for to be what they choose for themselves**
> **without any insistence that they satisfy you.**
> **—Wayne Dyer**

After reading about twenty couples experiencing successful marriages, we ask ourselves, *Did these couples have no domestic problems or conflict? Were they ever short of money? Did their children ever cause them problems? Were they ever ready to give up on marriage? Was it always smooth sailing?*

We all know the answers. The couples mentioned here are all imperfect, like the rest of us. Two imperfect people do not make a perfect couple! But it is great to note the flexibility they exercised.

There are three outstanding characteristics of the couples covered in this chapter.

1. Acceptance

Each couple has accepted one another's differences in their background and in their personalities. And let us face reality, these couples have had their differences. Their temperaments, their likes and dislikes, their energy levels, and one could go on and on with their differences. But in their marriages, the differences have not interfered with their love and devotion to each other.

> **My idea of an agreeable person is one who agrees with me.**
>
> **—Ubo Bohun**

I am thinking of a couple who celebrated their fiftieth wedding anniversary. each of them came from a very different home life. The husband was raised in a dysfunctional home, where his parents bickered and fought until they ended up in divorce court. He was raised in poverty and quit school at the age of fourteen. He had limited skills in interpersonal relationships. His wife was raised in a loving, peaceful home, where her parents manifested unity and understanding. She completed high school with excellent grades and went on to college through to graduation.

With such severe differences, one would not expect their marriage to work out. But it did. How? They did not allow their backgrounds and differences to get in the way of establishing a home where the children could be raised well and sense the love of their parents for each other.

2. Appreciation

Instead of emphasizing differences, the couples have appreciated what each spouse brought into the marriage. This became very clear as you read about the various ways they have appreciated what each spouse brought into the marriage. One was considerate for the variety of meals. Another appreciated the token ways their spouse would do little things like leaving a note on the mirror for her to see: "You are beautiful". One husband, to show his appreciation for his wife, sent her eleven roses with a note saying, "You are the twelfth."

Most of us fail all too often to express appreciation or consolation to those around us. Ben Franklin put his finger on it when he said, "We must give an account for every idle silence."

It is so easy to tell your wife that the meal was nice or to tell your husband that what he did for your parents was a fine thing. Perhaps you have heard about the remarkable operation that took place at a university teaching hospital. There a man received both a new heart and new lungs. It was a thrilling medical achievement. The patient and his wife were being interviewed. They mentioned that their brush with death brought a wonderful new appreciation for life into their hearts. They were excited about the privilege of living. Their love for one another just poured out. They were now living each moment with a special awareness of how precious it is. They savored it like a child rolls jelly around in his mouth before swallowing it.

The moral? Look for ways to show appreciation to your spouse again and again.

3. Affection

Reading about these twenty couples, their affection for each other comes through loud and clear. And that is an important part of married life. As you know, affection is much more than sex. Sex is an important part of marriage, but overall, it is perhaps only 15 percent. Sex is not a measure of love for our spouse. Affection is shown in the way we handle our helpmate in our attitude and in our aspiration for their love and devotion. It is to enjoy being alone with our spouse, without having to always engage in conversation. Affection has to do with the way we look at our spouse with a thankful heart. Solomon reminds us in Ecclesiastes chapter three that there is a time to show affection.

> **I would rather have the affectionate regard of my fellowmen than I would have heaps and mines of gold.**
>
> **—Charles Dickens**

Now, our personalities can influence the affection we have for our spouse. The way we were raised also can influence us. For instance, did we see real affection in our parents? Our daily mannerisms can have a part in how we show affection. Do you as a husband still open the car door for your wife? Do you as a wife go out of your way, at times, to give your husband his favorite dessert?

In displaying affection, we are not looking to be repaid. Rather, it is an expression of our feeling toward our spouse. In essence, affection grows out of an acceptance of who they are.

May the remarks of these twenty couples assist those who are planning to remarry.

# Wrap Up

In the final analysis, God has a plan for your life. It may or may not include a marriage partner. Regardless, it is important that you become the individual God would use to complete His will in others' lives.

## Think About This!

Which three couples would you like to emulate and why?

........................................................................

........................................................................

........................................................................

Can you suggest areas other than the ones mentioned here? Clarify.

........................................................................

........................................................................

........................................................................

........................................................................

........................................................................

........................................................................

........................................................................

........................................................................

........................................................................

........................................................................

........................................................................

........................................................................

........................................................................

........................................................................

# CHAPTER SIX

# Handling An Ex-Spouse

Ex-spouses come in all sizes and dispositions. The other day I attended a wedding where the bridegroom's former spouse was present with her new husband. When asked about her first marriage, she acknowledged without hesitation that they should never have married. She was strong enough to admit the reality of the situation. In another case, a professional got his secretary, nine years younger than himself, pregnant. She carried her baby without insisting on marriage. She recognized that their personalities would not work well together to form a good marriage. Was she resentful? No. Today, they are the best of friends, and she appreciates the woman he eventually married. The two cases above are the exception to the way things turn out with many ex-spouses. As Mary Jones says in her book *Stepmothers:*

> *I've never even met her, but I sense her everyday like an unseen, sinister presence in my home.*

Another spouse said about the ex-spouse:

> *She's not exactly an ex-wife. She's his other wife.*

An ex-spouse can try the most patient stepmother. She can bring the children to her ex-husband for the weekend and conveniently "forget" to include pajamas or some other article of clothing. This means that on Friday night the family must change their plans and go shopping for clothes instead. That's taxing! It would not be as hard to take if the children were to show some appreciation and give a word of thanks. Unfortunately, in many instances, the husband will not take a stand with his ex-wife and object!

> **He who gains victory over me is strong, but he who gains victory over himself is all-powerful.**
>
> **—Lso Tse**

Another possible difficulty is that of the stepchildren not recognizing or accepting the authority of their stepmother.

*I don't have to obey you! You are not my mother. I am going to tell my mother about you. You called me a spoiled brat. My mom will fix you.*

These things are hard to take, day after day, or even weekend after weekend. Of course, this is where the father must step in. But in many cases, he is afraid of taking too much action and risking his visiting rights with his children. However, his wife needs to insist he takes charge before the situation becomes more serious.

You can see the wisdom of holding a family meeting at the very beginning of the remarriage, before negative things begin to occur. In many cases where the second marriage does not work out, it is the action and behavior of the stepchildren that are to blame. It takes the wisdom of Solomon, as well as patience, tolerance, and a forgiving spirit to relate to many ex-spouses.

> **Stand up to your obstacles and do something about them. You will find that they haven't half the strength you think they have.**
> **—Norman Vincent Peale**

Not many have said to me what one ex-wife said about her husband:

> *I am so thankful to be divorced. How I ever married him is beyond me. But it is over now and I am glad.*

This ex-wife could not have cared less whether her former husband dated or remarried. She was through with him. Well, not quite. You see, they had two children. So they had to face each other on a fairly regular basis, at the children's birthdays and Christmas.

Ex-spouses also can create serious problems when their children have grown up and are preparing for marriage. One daughter wanted her father to give her away at her wedding. Her mother, who really had no time or love for her ex-husband, said to her daughter:

> *Well, Pam, your father did nothing for you. His support payments only came for a few months, until I went to court. Even then he stopped sending them after several months. He did nothing to help you in college. I really want nothing to do with him! I would rather have your older brother give you away.*

Now you can imagine the difficult situation in which the daughter finds herself. By having her father give her away, is she showing a lack of appreciation for what her mother has done for her over the years? On the other hand, her father did have a part in giving her life. This situation places a major responsibility on the daughter when she least needs it. The daughter needs to understand that she and her husband-to-be are about to form a new family unit. It is up to them to make the decision as to who will give her away. This also gives her an opportunity to exercise her independence. She has the opportunity to make her own decision, without being swayed by emotion or favoritism. After all, in the near future she will not be running back and forth to her mother to ask about what she should do in situations that arise. Let us suppose she does call upon her father to give her away. Will she hurt her mother? Perhaps. But this might also help her mother to accept the fact that the past is the past, and it must not interfere with what her grown children are doing today.

**As the sun makes the ice to melt, kindness causes misunderstanding, mistrust, and hostility to evaporate.**

**—Albert Schweitzer**

When there are children involved, there are various ways ex-spouses can make it difficult for the new family, if they choose to do so. A mother has custody of her six-year-old son throughout the week, and the father over the weekend. The arrangement is that dad picks up Johnny each Friday at 5:45 PM. The father gets out of work at 5:00 PM, so this gives him ample time to get his son. However, the father has not gotten over his marriage, and from time to time he attempts to frustrate his ex-wife. She called and asked him to be on time, since she had a friend coming to pick her up at 6:30. Well, she should never have called him, because he took advantage of an opportunity to hurt her again. That particular Friday he decided to work late and was not there to pick up his son until 7:00 PM. When he got to the house, he found his son waiting for him along with his ex-wife and her new date. Well, understandably, she was ready to blow steam, but could not with her new date there waiting. Never again when she had a date would she call him to ask him to be on time.

Actually, the previous situation is quite common among parents who come to pick up their offspring. What would you do if you were in their position? One mother had a fine solution. After her ex-husband was late several times, she phoned him and told him that if he was late the next time, she would take their sons to his parents' home, about an hour away, and he could pick them up there. Guess what? He was never late again! She did not argue with her ex. She did not make a scene. She simply told him in a direct way how she was going to handle the situation.

Wives can be a problem, too. One wife knew that after her children were picked up by her ex-husband, he would take them right home where his new wife would have dinner ready. The ex-wife still had not gotten over the divorce and was, at times, angry with her ex-husband. So one Friday at 4:30 PM, she took her children out to Pizza Pizza where they had their fill. Of course the meal included all the soda the children wanted. Well, when the father arrived at 5:30, he found the children full and certainly not ready to sit down to another meal. The ex-wife used this opportunity to hurt her ex-husband and his new wife.

**He that cannot forgive others breaks the bridge over which he must pass himself; for every man has need to be forgiven.**

**—Thomas Fuller**

There is also the ongoing problem of jealousy. The ex-husband is perceived to treat his new wife in a more favorable way.

> *He never gave me a necklace like that. He talked about us going on a cruise but it never happened. He never gave my parents a car!*

Feeling jealous over the way in which the new wife is treated can prolong the emotional struggle of the ex-wife and make things difficult, especially if the children not only hear it from their mom but also notice the differences themselves.

One father went to pick up his ten-year-old son and found the new husband of his ex-wife playing catch with him. This was too much for him emotionally, so he appealed to his ex-wife, asking her to ensure that their son and her new husband would not be playing together out front when he arrived. The ex-wife was quite understanding and saw to it that her new husband was not playing with their son at the time he was to be picked up. It is interesting to note that the father made his appeal in a gracious way, without complaining or showing anger. Love begets love and sometimes grace begets grace!

There are situations where a husband, in trying to hurt his wife while they are separated but not yet divorced, can actually hurt himself. In one case, the husband, to show his anger against his wife, dropped her name from their health insurance policy. Fortunately for him, she did not get sick. Otherwise, he would have been responsible for covering her medical costs, since they were still married.

Another serious problem is the separated spouses using their children to convey messages to each other. This often results in their offspring forming opinions about their parents, which are usually negative. One mother told her children while they were waiting for her ex-husband to pick them up,

> *You tell your father that the monthly support payment has not been received, and if I do not have it by this time next week, he will not have you for the weekend.*

Now the husband should have paid up, and paid up on time. However, it would have been much better if the ex-wife had called her ex-husband and threatened him personally, thus keeping their children out of the dispute. Doesn't the wife understand that in asking her children to relay the message, she is in essence telling them that their dad is no good and irresponsible! She also is saying indirectly that there are things they do not have because their father is late with his support. Fighting couples should keep their children in their thoughts and on their hearts. They should not involve them in their own domestic struggle.

**He who takes a child by the hand takes the mother by the heart.**

**—Danish Proverb**

Another serious problem with an ex-spouse arises when the individual is not willing to settle differences without developing high divorce fees. I have heard the following from a spouse facing separation:

> *Yes, I realize it is going to cost $5,000 to $10,000 to handle the settlement, but I would rather give it to my attorney than to my spouse!*

Such an attitude shows the depth of bitterness on the part of the spouse and an unwillingness to face reality. The pity is that when the divorce proceedings are all over, the spouse will recognize how foolish it was to have had such an attitude.

**Be ye angry, and sin not; let not the sun go down upon your wrath.**

**—Ephesians 4:26**

Many spouses struggle to get their former spouses not only to face reality but to accept it. John and Susan Anderson, both in their late fifties when they married, purchased a new residence. John was able to put in 35 percent of the cost and Susan 65 percent. Five years later, their marriage broke up and they put their house up for sale. Susan wanted 65 percent from the selling price but John said:

> *No way! We divide it fifty-fifty because it was our domestic residence, and we lived in it together.*

Well, you can hear Susan coming back with her answer:

> *John, that is not fair. You only contributed 35 percent to the purchase price and so that is all you should get from the selling price.*

Yes, it was brought to Susan's attention that the law would divide the sale of the house fifty-fifty, but Susan would not listen. And so it was back to the lawyers and to the court. Can't you see the lawyers laughing all the way to the bank! Someone might suggest that in a situation like this, Susan should request that a neutral mediator be employed. This they did, but Susan was so angry she would not accept the opinion of the mediator.

Correct

Actually, Susan is typical of people who are known for being unreasonable and self-centered. There is little one can do for such an individual with their unreasonable lifestyle. These people are so concerned about their own interests that they have difficulty seeing the other side of things. In Susan's case, her feelings were so raw and her anger so strong that she was not prepared to compromise or to accept the reality of the situation.

Sometimes an ex-spouse is really angry and wants to go to court. The spouse may present such a strong opinion that when the judge or mediator hears their side, judgment is given in their favor. However, there is usually difference between what people expect and what really happens. Judges are human, too, and do the best they can. However, they must abide by the law and not be influenced by the feelings or expectations of the people involved in the case. It is important for the spouse who is being verbally abused to understand that the other spouse is acting out of anger and frustration and to allow for this.

If all else fails, perhaps the new wife could visit the ex-spouse and try to reason with her. She should describe how the present situation with its arguments is really not helping anyone and is only prolonging the hard feelings. She should discuss the facts.

> *You are now divorced. I have now married your ex-spouse. Things cannot be changed or undone. Now, how can we make the best of it? As I look at the whole situation, I can see where I have made mistakes. These are the areas for which I accept full responsibility, and I am asking for your forgiveness. (Name the areas and try to major on the important points. Perhaps this will help the ex-spouse to examine themselves and note their mistakes as well.) Now with everything out in the open, let us decide to let the past be the past, because there are going to be many opportunities in the future where we will cross paths. When we celebrate family birthdays and special holidays, it would be great for the whole family to see us getting along. From this day forward, my commitment to you is to speak well of you both as an individual and as a parent. I would like for us to always have a friendly relationship, supporting each other. Now, what do you think? Perhaps you are thinking that it will never work. You could be right but there is no harm in giving it a try!*

Now, on an entirely different level, you could face an unexpected challenge. Your phone rings at seven o'clock in the evening. It is a call from an officer of the law, informing you that your ex-spouse has been involved in a serious auto accident and has been taken to a local hospital. You have been called because your name and phone number are still listed in your ex-spouse's pocketbook as the person and number to be phoned in case of an emergency. It had been there long before the divorce and was never updated. You still have the power of attorney! Now this situation gives you an opportunity to mend some fences and to bridge the gap made by the divorce. At the same time, your spouse will be very understanding of the situation as they realize the criticalness of the event in which you find yourself.

The same could be applied if your ex-spouse came down with a terminal illness. If the individual has not remarried and there are no living parents or siblings nearby, you will probably be more involved. You should do this in love, remembering you were once married to this individual. Doing good is always in season!

**Don't worry that children never listen to you, worry that they are always watching you.**
**—Robert Futchum**

It is important to bear in mind that when you marry a divorced spouse who has children, in one way or another, the ex-spouse will be part of the package you marry. Keep this in mind so that, if and when problems arise, you are somewhat prepared. This reality need not keep you from marrying the divorced spouse, but at the very least you have discussed it and to some degree have planned how the two of you will handle the problems as they arise. Think of some of the issues that could come up and plan how you will handle them.

The best way to handle issues is to establish a friendly relationship with the ex. You may not like them, and it might be a challenge to develop a solid understanding between the two of you, but it could save you from difficulties later on. Also, encourage each of the children to maintain a proper relationship with their biological parent. At the same time, you need to be careful what you say to your stepchildren about their biological parent.

**He who throws mud gets his hands dirty.**
**—Unknown**

Let's face it, to be married to a spouse with children from a previous marriage is not easy, but with patience and understanding, it can be a delight. Regardless of what the ex-spouse says about you, remember— exercise self-control and take the high road, which is always better. He who throws mud gets his hands dirty! If your relationship with an ex-spouse is negative, and you are planning to involve them in caring for the children while you take a holiday, have a back-up plan. For example, you and your spouse have scheduled a one-week cruise. The ex is going to care for the children. However, a few hours before your plane is to leave the ex calls to say that now, due to unforeseen circumstances, they will be unable to care for the children! What do you do with only hours to spare? This is where it is best to have a back-up plan should such a thing occur.

There are some ex-spouses who never do solve their problems. They go on and on talking about their misery and how terrible their spouse has been to them. Connie Abrons, a divorce researcher, calls these individuals "fiery foes," due to the hateful relationship they have with their ex-spouse. Court battles are the result, as well as mounting legal fees. What makes this situation very serious is that it involves the children. The last thing children want to see is their parents upset with each other. And when there is also physical violence, this becomes a major factor in decreasing the children's respect for their parents. It is much better for parents going through a marriage breakup to consider the children they brought into the world and to change their behavior accordingly. It has always been a mystery to me how two people can stand before me and exchange their wedding vows in the presence of God, their family, and friends and then sometime later, yell at their spouses and call them the vilest of names. And to make matters worse, in some cases they carry on this negative and immature behavior for years and years!

# Wrap Up

When dealing with an ex-spouse, you may be facing immaturity, jealousy, and a host of other emotional problems. It is important that you do not respond in the same way that you are being treated, but that you keep a steady head and maintain a balanced disposition.

## Think About This!

What additional counsel would you offer a spouse dealing with a difficult ex-spouse?

# CHAPTER SEVEN

## Developing a Blended Family

One of the major revolutions in family living today is the development of the blended family. This involves children who are being introduced to the new spouses of their parents and who are facing the new experiences and challenges of blending into a new family. Becoming a stepchild means living with new siblings and a new parent and getting to know new relatives, such as aunts and uncles. The blended family really introduces a whole new meaning to the word family.

Unfortunately, 65 percent of blended marriages do not last. This is largely due to the basic difficulties that inevitably arise out of blending two families. However, there are some excellent models of happy blended families.

> **You decide what it is you want to accomplish and then lay out plans to get there, and then you just do it.**
> **—Nancy Ditz**

Rob and Colleen Davis brought into their blended family seven children all under nine. Both were missionaries under Overseas Missionary Fellowship. Rob's wife had died of cancer, leaving him with four children. Colleen's husband was killed by terrorists on the mission field, leaving her with three children. After raising all seven, Rob gives this good word:

> A blended family will never be the same as a biological family, but it can be just as good.

Rob's only daughter, Beth, had a problem adjusting to Colleen, her stepmother. She felt she was betraying her deceased mother by showing affection to Colleen.

Both Rob and Colleen emphasized the importance of daily devotions.

**Do you really think you would be any less driven if you were single and had no children? I think not.**
**—Richard Exley**

Here is another account of an amazing blended family. Ruth Powers attended the same high school as her first husband, Chuck. They became serious about their future together, but Ruth did not want to marry Chuck unless he became a believer. Later on, he made a profession of faith and they proceeded to make plans for the wedding. Ruth's parents were not that pleased about the forthcoming marriage, but their daughter did not listen to them. She figured that Chuck was a new Christian and that she would be able to change him, when they were married.

Ruth was generally satisfied with her marriage. She was delighted to have four children and what she thought was a good marriage. However, in their nineteenth year, word reached her that Chuck, her husband, was having an affair with one of her best friends. This is how she described it:

> I was devastated, deeply hurt, guilt-ridden. I felt betrayed and deceived, not only by my husband but also by my friend. At first, I carried anger and bitterness towards both of them.

This situation was shocking to Ruth and also very disturbing to her family. When Chuck left her for this so-called friend of hers, Ruth had to go back to teaching since she still had her family to raise.

Even though being single for four years was not easy, Ruth was not looking for a new husband. At this time, one of her daughters was playing on the team at her school with another teenager, whose mother had died a year earlier. This girl's father had nine children and very much needed help in his home. The two single parents met at one of the school's functions. There was immediate chemistry between the two, and they started dating.

**The man who removes a mountain begins by carrying away small stones.**

**—Chinese Proverb**

Ruth, sensing that the romance was budding, drew up a list of things she wanted in a new husband. This is the way she described it:

> First, I did not want to aggressively look for a husband, but I believed if God wanted me to remarry, he would send someone to me without an effort on my part.

> Second, I thought if God wanted me to remarry, I would like my husband to be a committed Christian who would be a spiritual leader to my children and me.

> To be approved and loved by my four children.

> To love my children and understand and relate to them.

> To have a world-view, since I was ministering to international students.

> To be financially comfortable, not necessarily wealthy, but to be able to support my children and me.

Well, Marvin met all her requirements, but Ruth was taken aback to hear that this retired colonel from the army had nine children, five of them teenagers. Was she ready for such a challenge? As for Ruth's children, they immediately took to Marvin, and he won her over in the end.

At the time of their wedding, there were nine teenagers! Because Ruth had been single for four years, while Marvin had been single for one year with his children, they thought it would be wise to meet with a counselor several times before their wedding. This turned out to be a valuable experience. Together, they were able to look back on their past, as well as their present situation. The children profited much from this experience, too.

**Not everything bad comes to hurt us.**
**—Italian Proverb**

Before marrying, Ruth made the following resolutions:

First, I will not try to change Marvin in any way but accept him for who he is.

Second, I will not make mountains out of molehills. I will not let little things build up and ruin our relationship.

Third, I will try to put l Corinthians 13:4-7 into practice in my relationship with Marvin and his children.

It is of interest to note that Marvin assured Ruth that his first loyalty, next to the Lord, would be to her, not to his children. One serious mistake that Marvin and Ruth made was that, after the wedding, they moved into Marvin's house because it was larger. Neither Ruth nor her children ever felt at home there. Three years later, the couple had a house built that met the needs of their family.

Yes, there were times when the children had their differences, with their parents and with each other. But love won out and theirs is an excellent example of a blended family.

In raising their blended family, Ruth tells how Marvin emphasized immediate obedience from his children and how they would call him "Sir." This approach to discipline came from a life spent commanding soldiers. It was only natural that he would want the same respect from his children. However, Ruth's children tended to argue or debate with her, which caused his children to think that her children were disrespectful. On the other hand, Ruth's children never talked about their mother behind her back, whereas Marvin's children did complain to others about their dad. Neither Ruth nor Marvin played favorites when raising both his and hers.

Ruth said that she emphasized good table manners and good English grammar when speaking, whereas to Marvin these were not so important. So one can see that they had many things to work out when they brought the two families together. Yes, there were lots of frustrations on the part of both families, but the good news is that today they all get along very well. Ruth says, "I am close to all thirteen children but it took a lot of work."

**Treasure the love you receive above all. It will survive long after your good health has vanished.**
**—Og Mandind**

Dr. James Bray, in his book *Stepfamilies,* gives the results of a 1992 study on stepfamilies:

1. A stepfamily has its own natural cycle.
2. A stepfamily takes several years to develop into a family unit.
3. A stepfamily is at greatest risk during the first two years.
4. A stepfamily ultimately coalesces into one of three basic forms: neotraditional, romantic, or matriarchal.
5. A stepfamily must accomplish four basic tasks in order to succeed: integrating the stepfather into the child's life, creating a satisfying second marriage, managing change, and developing workable rules.
6. A stepfamily can heal the scars of divorce.

The previous section lists several areas of concern in building a blended family. Naturally, there is the temptation for the biological parent to favor his or her own children. After all, they are related to each other by blood, and so it would be easy to favor them over their spouse's children. On the other hand, reverse psychology also can come into play. This is where one favors the adopted ones in order to gain their acceptance. Neither approach should be used; as much as possible, husband and wife should seek to be neutral.

> **In this world there are only two tragedies. One is not getting what one wants, and the other is getting it.**
> **—Oscar Wilde**

Blending also can lead to difficulties in a family where a boy takes a sexual liking to his teenaged stepsister, and they have started practicing sex. There have been situations where the girl has become pregnant! An even more serious situation is where the stepfather begins to have sexual relationships with his teenaged stepdaughter. It may well be that the girl has seduced her stepfather; but, if she is underage, then it becomes a criminal event and should be reported to the authorities.

Actually, this experience of blending a teenaged girl into the family gives the stepfather an opportunity to demonstrate how a man treats a lady. He does this by the way in which he treats her mother and the respect he has for the teenage daughter and her privacy.

Boundaries can serve well in this home environment. The way the teenager dresses herself around the house and the way she speaks to her stepfather are all part of living respectfully in a family. Likewise, the stepfather must be careful how he talks with the teenaged stepchild, and how he touches her and his thoughts toward her must all come into consideration.

**In all things it is better to hope than to despair.**
**—Johann Wolfgang von Goethe**

Involving the children in planning the wedding service is a fine way to gain their cooperation and support. It also would be wise to have a trained counselor sit down with the children to answer their questions and to help prepare them for blended family living. The counselor should deal tactfully with some of the problems of the first marriage, if it ended in divorce, and set the tone for a good remarriage. In this situation, the counselor should remind the children of good experiences from the first marriage so that it is not all negative. Yes, there will be changes, but they can be for the good, if they are ready to accept them and move on with life and living.

Is it better for the biological parent to announce the marriage to all the children together or to take each of them aside, individually? Why not assemble the kids together as a family and announce what they already know or suspect? Should the new spouse be in on the gathering? It depends on how the parent feels the children are going to respond. Sometimes the biological parent can handle the response better, if it is negative. In this announcement, it is important to be positive and not to criticize the other biological parent. In fact, there is wisdom in reminding the children that they will still get to see and visit their other biological parent. However, you also want them to accept the new spouse as a loving stepparent. And no, they do not have to call them "Mom" or "Dad."

> **He who is not courageous enough to take risks will accomplish nothing in life.**
> **—Muhammad Ali**

This announcement will open the door for a conference with the new stepparent. Assure the children that the two of you will speak as one voice and that you both expect obedience and respect in the home. Assure them that allowances will continue as before, as well as visits to their other biological parent.

Seek to understand if and when one of your teenagers appears to be rebelling. It could perhaps be his way of showing independence or even of letting you know that you are not going to take the place of his biological mother. A teenager going through the breakup of his family is going through a very difficult experience, along with having to get his schoolwork done and keeping in touch with friends and family from prior to the divorce or move. In fact, a stepparent would be wise to build up the biological parent by showing love and consideration. This means that you will not seek to become the real parent, thus reducing the status of the biological parent.

As mentioned before, you may want to include the children in the wedding service. In this way they will sense that they are part of the new home. And it will be "new" with a stepparent living with them. Yes, there will be changes, but introduce them gradually. If you sense that there will be opposition from other family members involved in the wedding, or if you are not prepared to fund an expensive wedding if it is a large family, then plan a quiet service with just the immediate family.

Here is where a mutual counselor can help. He will remind the children that they will not be cut off from their biological parent. However, suggestions should be made as to how the children should deal with both sets of parents, including the extension of parental care.

It is vital to keep in mind the emotional, physical, and mental impact that a remarriage has on the children. They may have had to leave their former home behind them, along with their buddies, who in some sense were part of the family. This also might mean that they are now going to a new school and all that that involves. Another major change is the presence of a new parent in the home and not knowing what the future holds, especially with regards to their relationship with their own parent. It is almost like starting over in a new family. So, when dealing with stepchildren, handle with care, for they are fragile.

**Kind words can be short and easy to speak, but their echoes are truly endless.**

**—Mother Teresa**

As mentioned before, stepchildren are silently wondering what the future holds for them. Will the new spouse be like my biological parent? How often will I get to see my real parent? What about my grandparents? My cousins? How will life change for me?

This is where you can have a family study session. Begin with soft drinks and popcorn and bring out into the open new arrangements. Ask for their input as well. What kind of a family should we have? What about allowances? Schedules? Chores?

After discussing the issues that concern the children, you will want to discuss money matters. (This is a universal issue in remarriage.) The parents, by now, should have discussed how their money is going to be handled. Among other things, allowances for the children, as well as the chores they will be expected to carry out, should be discussed.

This is also the time to establish a weekly or biweekly family night. Plan supper around the food that the children enjoy, such as pizza or hot dogs. Set aside everything else, including television programs, sports, and other events, to discuss family activities, problems, and situations. The father needs to provide leadership here! What do you discuss at the family gathering? Go over the goals you have drawn up and decide if changes need to be made. Raise issues that will bring everything out into the open. Plan special events and deal with finances. Check your schedule and take note of special events coming up, such as a visit by grandparents or an uncle or aunt. Make sure this event happens on time and is not too long. Make it a lively and positive experience.

One important factor must be kept in mind, and that is to encourage the stepchildren, especially the teenagers. A positive word from a parent will go far in establishing confidence in your teenagers and getting support from them. You also will find that consistency is not always easy to maintain, but it sure pays off!

**In the middle of difficulty lies opportunity.**
**—Albert Einstein**

Yes, if there are stepchildren involved when blending families, make sure they understand the rules in the newly formed family. Do not get upset with or criticize the other parent. You are not responsible for what takes place elsewhere. It is great if you and the other parent can share the same expectations and are in agreement relative to rules, hours, and behavior.

It is interesting to note that, according to Ericka Lutz in her book *Step-parenting,* a deceased spouse is easier on the marriage, but harder on your relationship with the children. A deceased parent is bigger than life and is a saint who did no wrong!

Often children have had liberties in their previous home that they do not have in the blended family. They will make comparisons. You come back with the statement: "But in our home we do it this way." There is no need to argue about the matter or discuss it any further. Again, you are setting boundaries, and the children will live with them, once they are explained to them.

When you are in a serious dispute with your stepchildren, remember that it is wise to take the high road. Do not use terms or call them names that you will later regret.

Ericka Lutz suggests that when resolving family conflicts you use "I" statements rather than "You." It is best not to bring up the past, but to stay with the present. Get away from using general terms, such as never, always, and all.

> **Write it on your heart that every day is the best day of the year.**
>
> **—Ralph Waldo Emerson**

In the busy schedule of caring for stepchildren, it is important that the couple take time for each other. Whether it be a date night without the children or a closed door to your bedroom, it is important that you have time to talk and cuddle together. Actually, this will help you as a stepparent! Many spouses find that a spouse with biological children at home will give considerable free time to them, often taking away from the time spent with the married spouse. This creates resentment and does not make for a solid marriage. This is why some women will wait till their suitor's children have grown up before they marry!

Again, Dr. Bray in his findings suggests that there are three cycles to a marriage involving a stepfamily. The first one lasts about two years. During this time, you all are getting to know each other. It involves stress and tension as you do so.

The second cycle runs from year three to year five. Reality has set in, and the members of the family are more realistic about each other.

The third cycle is from the fifth year to the ninth. Stress is again present as rules are questioned and authority is tested. The moral of the story is that you exercise much patience until you sense that the members of the family have somewhat accepted the blended home.

The question often arises as to how much the children should know as to why the parents separated and later divorced. It is better that the children hear the details from their parents rather than from a relative or even from a neighbor. It is beneficial for them to hear what the problems were from both sides, mom's and dad's! Let them know where you realize you were in the wrong so that they can see you are human, too!

One advantage to all of this is that the children, to some degree, will begin to understand why their parents broke up and that the breakup did not involve them. It is good for them to know that they were not to blame for the family domestic problems.

> **You will find as you look back upon your life that the moments you have truly lived are the moments when you have done things in the spirit of love.**
> **—Henry Drummond**

Furthermore, it is an education for their own future marital relationships. It also corrects any untruths that they may have heard about their parents. In addition, it gives the children the assurance that their parents love them, want the best for them, and can trust them. This is so meaningful. Tell it to the children in a family setting so that they can hear the same reasons and explanations.

# Wrap Up

---

Develop positive relationships with blending families and encourage them. It is important that parents involved with the establishment of a blended family do extensive homework both in reading and planning.

## Think About This?

Do you have family members building a blended family? If so, what are you doing to assist them?

# CHAPTER EIGHT

## Living Through A Difficult Marriage

For many couples divorce is not in the picture! True, legally they have grounds for divorce, but for one reason or another, they decide to endure their situation, regardless of how difficult it may be. Many consider divorce, but when they look at all the angles, they feel it would be better to remain married.

In a divorce situation, you may face many challenging and inconvenient problems. Consider the matter of dividing up the "stuff." If the marriage has lasted five years or longer, the drawers and closets and the house in general are filled with clothes, jewelry, and a thousand other items. Who gets what?

A financial crisis often accompanies divorce. Now, in place of one residence, there are two. You have to have two of everything. It all must be paid for, and if there is only one salary, this can become a serious problem.

As a married couple, you might have been living in a small but comfortable house with some green space around it. Now, you are faced with living in a two- or three-room apartment and possibly having to share a bathroom! "No, thank you," you say!

At least when married, you had some meals together as a couple. Now, in singleness, unless there are children, you eat with the daily news on the television. As far as your friends are concerned, the breakdown of your marriage is forcing some of them to make a decision as to whose side they will take in the dispute. Even close friends, due to pressure from their spouses, may desert you.

Besides, perhaps 90 percent of the time the marriage is fine and the two of you live in a relatively peaceful situation. It is the other 10 percent, where there is heartache and one situation after another, that is a problem to handle. Yes, you feel trapped! You wish and you wish for a remedy or for some relief, but you see none in sight. Where can you go? What can you do?

> **The art of being wise is the art of knowing what to overlook.**
>
> **—William James**

In this chapter, we are dealing with addictions. They can take many forms. An addiction is simply a compulsion to carry out what can be negative behavior to the point of self-destruction. Common addictions would include alcoholism, drug abuse, gambling, sex, and compulsive spending.

Of course, if there are children in the marriage, the problem is 100 percent worse. Depending on their age, they may or may not understand the seriousness of the problem. The following are real situations, with some suggestions as to how to live through, with, and in them.

What is an alcoholic spouse? A simple answer would be an individual who drinks alcohol to excess, where he or she loses control but goes on drinking anyway. They can have hangovers along with severe headaches. They can lose self-control and take it out on the one closest to them—their spouse. They can spend hard-earned money that was set aside for food or furniture or other family needs. They can get behind in paying monthly bills and run up major financial debt.

At times, they can be mild in temperament and at other times wild with anger. When the individual is not in full control, he or she can be absolutely destructive, taking valuable glassware and dishes and dropping them or throwing them against the wall. Many at times will strike their spouse or child without provocation. Some tend to blame others for their own stupidity. Talking to them will do little good.

Damage caused by people who cannot control their consumption of alcohol is considerable. An even greater tragedy is the potential loss of life by driving under the influence of alcohol. It is estimated that about 62 percent of our North American population drink. No one has yet determined the number of alcoholics. The sad thing is that this is a lifelong problem unless it is checked by professionals. An excellent description of alcoholism is stated in *Alcoholism*. (33)

> Alcoholism is a compulsion to drink that leads to a breakdown in the victim's ability to function. He suffers more than heartburn or social embarrassment. Alcohol, for the alcoholic, is a lethal poison, a destroyer of the person's ability to lead anything resembling a normal person . . . the alcoholic's body comes to depend on alcohol almost as much as it depends on oxygen and food.

The book of Proverbs gives keen insight into this topic of drinking alcohol. Chapter 20, verse 1 states:

> Wine is a mocker, strong drink is raging: and whosoever is deceived thereby is not wise.

Proverbs 23:21a points out that

> The drunkard and the glutton shall come to poverty.

So you have made the decision to endure your marriage to an alcoholic spouse. Given this, do not nag or stir up a verbal dispute. It will only make things worse for the two of you. Your spouse is already down and probably depressed, so there is little value in pushing them any lower.

I take it that you are a total abstainer! After all, you cannot expect your spouse to cease drinking, if indeed, you bring alcohol home or even drink socially. Some spouses try to anticipate when their partner is going to drink and then plan around it. It is wise to make your friends aware of the situation, so that they will not drink when the individual is present.

Multitudes have been helped through Alcoholics Anonymous. Their goal is to help alcoholics become total abstainers! They seek to help drinkers handle sobriety. Alcoholics Anonymous has several general principles that you can put into practice, as stated in their book on alcoholism.

1. Children, as much as possible, should not see the drunken behavior.
2. The alcoholic must face the consequences of his or her behavior.
3. Don't make an excuse for him or her.
4. Don't bail him or her out of jail.
5. Don't try to control his or her behavior.

There is hope for the alcoholic when you realize that alcohol is a choice and not a disease.

What husband wants to live with a wife who is giving her body to others, whether it be in a heterosexual or a homosexual relationship? The same question can be addressed to a wife. But there are those who feel trapped and would rather endure their spouse's extramarital relationships than end the marriage. They are praying, hoping, and longing that such relationships will end—and end soon.

One problem is that the relationship with one person might end, but within a short span of time the individual takes up with another person. Of course the result of this kind of behavior is one of disease!

Let's face it: there are womanizers who insist on having relationships outside of marriage. One can appreciate the difficulty of living in such a situation. It becomes an especially serious problem when a pregnancy results from the extramarital relationship. Then there are years of support ahead. If their budget is already in the red, imagine the headache facing the married couple. Furthermore, the father will have visiting rights and will be involved in raising two families. One would think that people would turn away from such relationships. However, if you do not have a solid relationship with your spouse, which can result in a lack of security, a third party may enter and will do immense damage to your marriage.

The Bible illustrates this form of betrayal in the book of Hosea. The prophet Hosea takes Gomer to be his wife. Then follow her acts of adultery. Yet Hosea loves and keeps her. Of course God was using all this as an illustration of how Israel had been unfaithful to Him.

> **What we do today, right now, will have an accumulated effect on all our tomorrows.**
> **—Alexander Stoddard**

It has been my experience in working with these kinds of situations that little can be done as long as the third party is in the picture. The chemistry is so strong that the third party takes the place of the spouse in the marriage. There is little sense in lecturing and scolding. You must be strong and keep yourself attractive and positive. Watch your weight! Your tongue! Your actions! No, your position is not hopeless. People can change, and you could be the means by which this might happen.

Are there areas where the two of you have not worked together? Are you able to plan as a couple and set up goals for your marriage? Or has it all been one-sided! In a marriage, both the husband and the wife like to have a meaningful part in the decision-making. At times, one partner might have to change their way of thinking (and speaking) from "We are going to do . . ." to "What do you think we should do?" Show grace and a forgiving spirit so that the offending individual will come to realize what real love is all about.

It is very hard to wake up in the morning not knowing what mood your spouse will be in. Some mornings, perhaps with the sun shining and the birds singing, your spouse will be as happy as a lark. It will be a fun day indeed. You might even go on a picnic or do something special. On another day, your spouse will want to remain in bed, perhaps with an exploding headache or just feeling sickly. With no desire for conversation, the individual desires to be left alone. Yelling, scolding, and criticism will get you nowhere.

Is such a disposition genetic or the result of circumstances? Even older people in their fifties, sixties, and seventies still can have mood swings that are the result of negative childhood experiences.

**A sad soul can kill you quicker, far quicker, than a germ.**

**—John Steinbeck**

Imagine a gifted nurse with a compassionate concern for others, yet she herself has difficulty maintaining a balanced emotional life. In fact, if she stops taking her medication, she feels it and will soon develop a severe depression. When she was eight years old, her brother, six years older, started sexually touching her. This went on for six years, until finally she told him to stop it or else she would tell their mother. But the damage had been done. He had robbed her of one of the most precious gifts God has given us. Not only that, but society failed her too. Medical doctors did not give her proper medications. She was referred to a professional psychologist, and he had her sitting on his lap! You and I would be in a deep depression, too, if we had been treated in the same way.

Folks with this kind of stress tire quickly. Almost everything becomes like a mountain to climb. Their equilibrium is off-balance, which might last a short or long period of time. This can bring on anxiety, anger, depression, or sexual isolation, and can lead to other problems as well. Such an individual tends to be self-focused, because he or she is forced to think in personal terms. As such, their energy is used up and they are not really able to minister to others, especially to members of their family.

How does one, who desires to maintain a good marriage, handle or live with such an individual? The suggestion is to stay away from quarrelling as much as possible. Remind yourself that this is really not the one you married! Carefully check to see that the medication is being properly taken. Instead of saying, "We are going to do this," say "Would you like to do this?" Bring the spouse into the decision-making. Ignore negative behavior as much as possible.

# 4—The Gay Spouse

Why would some people in the gay movement marry a heterosexual without telling their spouse of their sexual preference? Probably if they did, the marriage would be called off. There have been couples who have been married for ten, twenty, and even forty years before an individual has come out of the closet. You can imagine the problems this leads to. The other spouse does not understand and is really disgusted. If there are children, what does this mean to them? How does one counsel them? How can you protect them? Can you imagine the questions going through their heads? Will the marriage stay intact or will there be a separation? Many desire to avoid a divorce, so they stay in the marriage and make the best of a bad situation.

Will there be changes in the marriage relationship? Yes, the gay spouse should have medical examinations. The couple will sleep in different beds. The "straight" spouse will seek to monitor the other, as far as extramarital affairs are concerned. Before the one spouse came out of the closet, things were fairly normal. But now all that has changed. Trust has become an issue.

**Satan does not here fill us with hatred of God, but with forgetfulness of God.**
**—Dietrich Bonhoeffer**

This leads us to ask how you can maintain the marriage under such circumstances. There is no value in belittling the spouse or scolding. Yes, you will want to establish some guidelines as to who can be invited for a meal or for an overnight. This you do with a cooperative spirit. Actually, with the trend toward accepting same-sex marriages, homosexuality is being recognized in some places as normal behavior. This is causing increased problems for spouses who want nothing to do with it.

If a grown child in the family adopts a homosexual lifestyle, it increases the burden to accept and live with the gay spouse. I have seen grown siblings divided, when one of them takes up the lifestyle of living with a gay partner. It can come to the point where the family members are so divided they will have little to do with one another.

In the final analysis, it will take considerable patience for the couple to continue to accept one another and to maintain the marriage.

Yes, there are people who are workaholics! Some like being a workaholic because they appreciate the recognition received from being so dedicated. Others really are unable to control their schedules and do not appreciate the time they have to give. Their spouses are not happy about it either, since they married each other because they wanted to spend a lot of time together. The children do not like it, as they would rather have time to play with their parents and do things together.

The average son or daughter could not care less if a parent has a high and important position. Children are living in the "now," and "now" is the time that they want this busy workaholic parent around. Five or ten years from now, they will be out on their own. In many cases, these grown children will not have time to set aside their personal activities to sit down and visit with their overworked parent. After all, where did they learn to be so busy?

> **Possibly the greatest malaise in our country is our neurotic compulsion to work.**
> **—William McNamara**

It is true that some occupations require more time than others. Medical personnel, who are on call, must be ready for emergencies. Clergymen have long hours preparing messages and counseling. Realtors work day and night to succeed. I have known realtors who have had customers sign papers after midnight! Citizens elected to public office are on call twenty-fours hours a day. Chief executive officers of large corporations receive bonuses of millions of dollars for sacrificing their home lives to get the job done.

Now you can see why this can lead to a serious domestic problem. How does a spouse plan dinner not knowing if anyone will be there to eat it? Or, how can you plan a social evening if there is uncertainty as to whether the co-host will be able to be there. Is the other spouse always to give away the leftover ticket to the concert or to a sporting event?

Now, mind you, the workaholic spouse will come up with acceptable excuses! Would you want that girl to die because of the party you had planned for tonight? Would you want me to leave Hank and Janet in the midst of their domestic dispute in order to attend the church social?

Would you want me to miss out on the commission of selling a half-million dollar property? There is no problem coming up with reasonable excuses. The problem is an unwillingness to be dispensable. Others can handle the emergency, too, but it is hard, sometimes, to let go.

It would appear that to many workaholics, their vocation has become their avocation. To many workaholics, work is fulfilling a personal need; and as such, it is worth giving it the extra time and effort.

So the spouse is willing to keep the marriage together. That is commendable. Criticism and scolding will not work. Pleading and begging will not do a lot of good. Continue to exercise patience, compassion, and understanding. Longsuffering is never out of season. People do change. People can change. It may be your lot to plan social events knowing that your spouse might not be there, and so you plan accordingly. If there is a graduation or special event involving a member of the family, put it on the calendar as soon as possible and in a mild way talk about the event well ahead of time.

Why some married people continue to live together in a home where there is physical abuse is hard to understand. Of course, the abuser will swear that it will never happen again. Even if he puts his hand on ten Bibles, something will come and set off the fuse, and the blows will come! Both husbands and wives are abusers, although the majority are men. These people eventually find out that their behavior does not satisfy them.

Now we need to keep in mind that the physical abuser will start with verbal attacks. When you sense what is coming, you try to calm things down. If, for example, the spouse says that you do not understand, ask questions. What is it that I do not understand? Asking for specific examples will give the abuser the feeling that you are listening. In the midst of the verbal attack, if possible, keep calm and try to hear him out. Now, if you find that some of the things he says about you are true, admit it and ask for forgiveness. At least you are responding to his rage. However, to tell him that he should not be angry is to pass judgment on his feelings, and no one likes that.

> **To triumph fully, evil needs two victories, not one. The first victory happens when an evil deed is perpetrated; the second victory, when evil is returned. After the first victory, evil would die if the second victory did not infuse it with new life.**
>
> **—Miroslav Volf,**
> ***The End of Memory***

Try talking on a day when things are great between the two of you. Suggest to your spouse that you would like to discuss a very serious problem so that you may hear what he has to say. Tell him you know that he loves you and that you both desire to make a great marriage. Let him also know that you are afraid of him. As long as there is physical abuse, our marriage cannot be what it could be and should be. Ask what his home was like. Did your father ever hit your mother? (You will find that in a large percentage of marriages where there was physical abuse, the son carries it on into his own marriage.) Assure him that you are not thinking of divorce, but rather trusting the physical abuse will cease. Ask him what he would like you to do the next time you sense he is going to strike you.

Another way to deal with the abuse is to tell your husband that you are not seeking a divorce, but, as of now, all physical abuse must stop. Tell him that the next time he strikes, the police will be called and he will be taken away in handcuffs. Let him know that you will not bail him out. He will have to spend the night in jail. Remind him that most likely he will be forced by the law to take a course on controlling his temper. Finally, let him know that are glad that you can talk this out.

I have seen this work, and the couples who have done this have grown in their marriages. The important thing is to bring this subject up for discussion at the right time, when no one is rushed and you have time to talk it through.

Finally, keep in touch with family members, siblings, friends, and even neighbors. You may want to get involved with a self-help group that can support you in improving your marriage. Keep your physical, moral, and spiritual strength up. Remember, God is on your side. Prayer does work. And people can change, even physical abusers.

There are three ways some couples handle their finances: miserly, foolishly, and frugally. If your spouse is one of the former, you will have serious financial problems, which will most likely lead to tensions in your marriage. On the one hand, there will be a hoarding of funds and the couple will stop buying what is necessary. On the other hand, money will be used to purchase unnecessary items, resulting in a shortfall to purchase items that are necessary.

Mark Samson is a schoolteacher, who from an early age started to hoard his allowances. Now as a grown adult, Mark is reluctant to purchase for his family unless it is absolutely necessary. His wife would like to go to another area for a medical treatment, but Mark forbids it, as there is no guarantee it will work. Yet the couple have thousands of dollars set aside for retirement.

> **In this world, it is not what we take up but what we give up that makes us rich.**
> **—Henry Ward Beecher**

Far too many couples have credit card debt. Their credit card statement arrives showing the minimum payment of perhaps fifteen dollars, although the actual balance is eighteen thousand dollars. Now some credit card companies will charge 18 to 19 percent interest. Furthermore, interest is charged from the date of each purchase. You can see why companies are anxious for customers to use their credit cards. Actually, some companies make more money on their cards than on the products they sell.

Life can be miserable if your spouse is careless, or even stupid, with money. You will be forced, perhaps, to work overtime or even get a second job to make ends meet. Stormie Omartian, in her book *Praying Through the Deeper Issues of Marriage,* says:

> The stress caused by spending foolishly, making unwise investments, and accumulating debt with never enough money to pay it off is beyond what any marriage can tolerate. If two people are going to live together successfully, they have to come to an agreement about how money is earned, spent, saved, given, and invested.

In recent days, several religious leaders have utilized the Ponzi scheme. Back in 1926, Charles Ponzi, a swindler, got people to invest and then paid them off using other people's money. In this way, he encouraged larger and greater risks. It is so important to stay away from investments that sound too good to be true. Also, get out of debt as soon as possible and stay that way!

How does one handle a difficult marriage where money is a prime factor? One spouse needs to sit down with the other spouse and together they draw up a budget. If one spouse is not agreeable, perhaps you will need to present a challenge. Are we going to remain married or not? Yes, it is that serious!

In drawing up a budget, the husband and wife need to keep an account of every penny spent for a period of sixty days. They will be surprised to see where the money has been used. What happens when your revenue is short of what your disbursements are? This is where you cut out unnecessary items: eating out daily, coffee breaks, alcohol, cigarettes, movies, and other things. It is absolutely necessary that your disbursements balance with your revenue. Otherwise you will always be in debt.

Yes, two can live together in a financially troubled marriage, providing you are willing to make the necessary adjustments. Dennis and Barbara Ralney had to make severe adjustments, as Barbara was raised in a country club setting while Dennis had a rural upbringing in Missouri. When they were engaged, Dennis went to buy a wedding gift for his wife. Barbara chose a pattern called "Old Master." He asked the price, and the clerk replied, "It's 59.99." Dennis thought it was for the setting but of course it turned out to be something like $20.00 for a knife! You can imagine the frank discussion they had, but they were able to reach a compromise. Today, they are leaders in the field of domestic counseling.

Couples need to understand money lifestyles, of which there are four, and the one by which they choose to live.

1. A couple can choose to live above their means. They will continue to spend more than their revenue. A divorced mother asked me about her finances, as her father would have nothing to do with her and her mother had died. Her divorce left her broke, which is not uncommon. Her remuneration was limited and her credit card debt exceeded twenty thousand

dollars. She had three choices: declare bankruptcy, tear up her credit cards, or marry. She was fortunate, as she found a man who proposed to her!

2. A couple can live at their means. You spend what you take in. There are no savings. No goals established. No plans. They are living from hand to mouth.

3. A couple can live within their means. Here they give consideration for their needs today and planning for tomorrow as well.

4. A couple can live below their means. This is not a typical choice many make. It calls for discipline and a deliberate choice. For these folks, they have a higher purpose for living. Many are blessed because of their support.

When I was in charge of church planting for my denomination, raising funds was important. I recall one elderly couple living out west in the oil country. Their home was humble indeed, including their furniture. Yet all around them, oil was coming from the ground. Wealth. They had it, but most of it went to missions. I always came away with a large gift for church planting.

# Wrap Up

In the final analysis, I believe couples in difficult marriages can work things out if the husband seeks to please his wife and the wife her husband. It all comes down to the relationships they have with each other and whether they are going to honor God in their marriage.

# Think About This!

Of the severely troubled marriages mentioned, which one, in your judgment, would be the most difficult to handle? What counsel would you offer?

# CHAPTER NINE

# Married People Can Have Significant Lives

The marriage ceremony was actually beyond their expectations. And the reception that followed went so well. The bride's brother and the bridegroom's brother both gave fine speeches at the reception. The honeymoon—well, it was great! But now the married couple is back home, somewhat in the same routine as before, except there are now two in the apartment, a husband and a wife, and that makes a difference.

Now, with a new marriage what does life hold for them? Well for one thing, life can be significant! How? The Bible gives us some guidelines in Psalm 90. This is a prayer of Moses, the servant of the Lord. He was an old statesman when he wrote this, probably around the age of one hundred. As Carl Lungquist said:

> We can learn much from this elderly statesman who was
> used by God to bring the children of Israel out of slavery
> to the Promised Land.

In this prayer, Moses has focused on the theme of *life*. He actually states three things about life.

Have you noticed the two ways Moses describes the shortness of days? First, he gives us a contrast between the eternal nature of God as compared to the brevity of our days. Secondly, he illustrates that brevity in verses four to six. In verses one and two, he talks about God being from everlasting to everlasting. Earlier Moses declared in Psalm 46:1,

> God is our refuge and strength, a very present help in trouble.

In our day of rapid change, it is a problem to grasp the concept of an eternal God, the unchanging One. Many have compared this attribute of God with that of a ring, where there is no beginning and no ending.

**Life is short, try to savour every moment.**
**—Karen Kain**

Moses also talks about the brevity of a man's life through illustrations in verses four to six. He talks about a thousand years as being like a day. He talks about the sudden flow of rushing water in a flood. He talks about grass and how quickly it withers. As parents, how often did we ask our teenagers to mow the lawn in the morning and by nightfall, the cut grass had turned a golden brown! Life is like that!

**Life moves pretty fast. If you don't stop to enjoy it**
**sometimes, it will pass you by.**
**—Ferris Bueller**

Yes, life is short. A number of years ago when I was getting underway as pastor in a new church, an elder who was in his early eighties asked me to visit his mother on her birthday. I was not sure whether he was joking, but I did go and was shocked to find out it was her one hundred fourteenth birthday. I remember how she ate two pieces of birthday cake and drank five cups of tea. She was born back in the 1880s, and yes, to her it was as yesterday! Life is short.

Not only is life short, but it also has been sinful. In verse seven, Moses talks about the anger of God. Why would God be angry? Well, he made the Garden of Eden for man's benefit. In the garden there was nothing else Adam could ever want. Yet, he disobeyed God. He questioned the authority of God. He went against the command that was clearly given.

**Our outward act is prompted from within and from the sinner's mind proceeds the sin.**

**—Matthew Prior**

In verse eight, Moses reminds himself that there are no secret sins man can hide from God. My wife has said to me several times, "I can read you like a book." Well, we men know that just is not so. Our wives think they know us well, but what human being can really know the inner springs of a man's heart? The reality, of course, is God! As our Creator, He knows our *secret sins*. Let us be clear about what the definition of sin is. It is more than a mistake or a slip of the tongue. It is actually rebellion against God. We must call sin by the same name that God does. As Anne Graham Lotz says in *Life Is Just Better With Jesus,*

> You and I often play games with the names we call sin. For example, we call the sin of unbelief, worry. We call the sin of lying, exaggeration. We call the sin of fornication, safe sex. As long as we switch the labels on sin to make it seem less serious, we are being dishonest with ourselves and with God.

In verses ten and eleven, Moses describes the result of our sin. There is labor and sorrow and ultimately death. The apostle Paul reminds us of this in Romans 6:23:

> For the wages of sin is death; but the gift of God is eternal life through Jesus Christ our Lord.

And this is why Jesus Christ went to the cross on our behalf, as we read in 1 Corinthians 15:3, 4:

> For I delivered unto you first of all that which I also received, how that Christ died for our sins according to

the scriptures; and that He was buried, and that He rose
again the third day according to the scriptures.

And so we acknowledge that life is short and that it has been sinful.
As the Anglican prayer book says:

We have done those things we ought not to have done, and
we left undone those things we ought to have done.

But still, after all is said and done, can there be meaning to life? Can
life still be significant? Psalm 90 gives a resounding, "Yes." But how? What
can a married couple do to have a significant life and marriage? This is
where we bring in the last six verses of Psalm 90.

In these verses, Moses gives a six-fold prescription of how life can be significant. In other words, follow this procedure and you will find the real meaning of life. Yes, this is an excellent way to add meaning to our lives.

1. Priorities—Verse 12

*Numbering our days* means we will establish a priority with the way in which we use our time. Now, whenever an item is in short supply, we consider how we can make the best use of what is left. A housewife, in seeking to make her grocery money go further, takes a list of things to buy with her when she goes shopping. She has prioritized her needs. A salesman with several calls to make will line up the addresses, so as not to retrace his steps. He has prioritized his deliveries. You and I cannot read every book that is printed. We decide what subjects interest us and we seek those out.

In the same way, because our time on earth is limited, we need to use it wisely. What better way to do so than to prioritize our days. Many couples, at the close of a year, will plan and establish goals for the new year. This is great teamwork, as the couple has set targets in mind and has established ways to reach them. Not only do we prioritize our time, but our money, for money, in the final analysis, is time!

Many of us are collectors of stuff! Our drawers are filled with stuff. Our shelves are filled with stuff. The garage is overflowing with so much stuff that it is not possible to park a car. Isn't that so? What are we going to do with this stuff? We men have one hundred neckties, but only one neck! If we live to be two hundred, we still will have ties we have not used. The older we get, the more we ask ourselves if we really want an item before making a purchase.

Another important area that must have priority is our marriage. The spouse we married needs quality time. The children we brought into the world need quality time. It has been my experience that one must plan time in our schedules for this. No, we do not have time, unless we plan and make it a priority.

Have you heard about the professor in social studies who illustrated the importance of giving your spouse first place? He had an empty large jar, and he filled it with rocks until they were showing above the top. He asked the class if the jar was full. They agreed it was. He next got a bag of small pebbles and they went slipping down between the rocks. Again he asked the class, "Is the jar full?" The class agreed that it was. The teacher next pulled out a bag of very fine sand and proceeded to fill the jar. The sand like the pebbles again just slid down between the rocks. Again the jar was filled. Or was it? He asked the class. Yes, the jar was full. The teacher next got a jug of water and started pouring it into the jar until it spilled over the rim. Now the jar was really full. He went on to say that the big rocks represented a spouse, and the spouse had to fill the jar first. If you put in the pebbles, sand, and the water, which represent work, sports, and other things, first, there would not be room for the big rocks. Giving your spouse time and room for developing and maintaining your relationship is an important priority.

Life starts to become significant when we establish priorities with our time and money, recognizing the important place of a spouse in marriage.

2.  Prayer—Verse 13

Here in verse thirteen, Moses pleads for the presence of God. In his prayer life, he yearns to sense the reality of God listening and hearing the cry of his heart. Life takes on significance when we meet with God and sense His presence by our side.

Max Lucado tells about visiting an elderly church member who was in the hospital. He noticed that one of the chairs in the room was turned and asked the meaning of it.

> Well, pastor, when I pray, I visualize Jesus sitting in the chair, listening and responding.

Several days later, the elderly man's daughter went to visit her father and found him kneeling by the chair. He had passed on while praying, but he had sensed the presence of God in his room. Prayer was not just repeating words and requests, but close communion with the Creator.

Many married couples like to have a daily time with the Lord. Life continues to become significant when, around the breakfast table in the morning or the dinner table at night, the two take a Bible, read a portion, and follow it up with a time of prayer. Faith becomes so meaningful when a couple practices the presence of God.

**And help us, this and every day, to live more nearly as we pray.**
**—Thomas Fuller**

Can you understand what praying Hyde meant when he said he was afraid, while praying, of reaching out and actually touching the person of the Godhead. Prayer was so meaningful to him. Sensing the presence of God in prayer continues to add significance to life.

3. Providence—Verses 14 and 15

The human mind cannot make sense of verse fifteen:

Make us glad according to the days wherein thou hast afflicted us, and the years wherein we have seen evil.

The only way to understand this is to recognize the providence of God. A married couple will experience many difficulties in life. However, when they recognize that God is in control, then life, in spite of all its hardships, takes on significance. Many do not understand why certain things happen to one and not to the other. Why did one get cancer? Why was the other hurt as a bystander? Why was one passed over for a raise?

**God allows us to experience the low points of life in order to teach us lessons we would not learn any other way.**
**—C.S. Lewis**

Some Christians ask why this problem or sickness happened to them. In reality, shouldn't it happen to them? The rain falls on the godly farm owners as well as the farms of people who never attend a church service. The couple with faith will rest in the assurance that God is in control of their lives.

**Smooth seas do not make skillful sailors.**
**—African Proverb**

Many Christian couples will talk about an accident or a problem that they have had and wondered why it happened. Later, they find that God brought something good out of the incident. This is where faith becomes practical and meaningful.

Again, the providence of God continues to bring significance into the home of a married couple when it is recognized that He is in control!

4.   Positveness—Verse 16

This verse emphasizes the call to have a spirit that is in contrast to a negative frame of mind. Someone has said it well:

> I would rather be on the construction crew as over against
> the demolition crew.

Verse 16 is excellent for reminding parents to be careful about criticizing servants of the Lord in the presence of their children. For that matter, regarding speaking in a negative way about any believer, Moses says in so many words,

> God, you are doing so much for the children of Israel.
> Help me to talk about that and not about the failures of
> some of our leaders.

If a young Christian disappoints you, refrain from criticism. Pray for him instead. Or in a quiet orderly way, make a point to sitting down with the individual and talking about your concern. That individual probably will give your words more attention, since the correction is done quietly and in a loving spirit. Yes, life continues to increase in significance when we seek to be positive in our relationship with others.

**I don't believe in pessimism.**
**—Clint Eastwood**

5.   Pattern—Verse 17A

Notice how Moses frames the following thought.

> And let the beauty of the LORD our God be upon us.

This is a great truth that the beauty, the grace, and the love of God are somehow manifested in our lives. How could any couple have a better relationship than one in which each radiates Jesus Christ in their lives!

Nothing can come between them when they so reflect the presence of God.

> **Do not let what you can't do interfere with what you can do.**
>
> **—John Wooden**

And what is such a life like? What visible manifestations should we see in such godly individuals? The qualities of a life lived for God are found in Galatians 5:22, 23. Paul lists the fruit of the Spirit as:

> Love.
> Joy.
> Peace.
> Patience.
> Kindness.
> Goodness.
> Faithfulness.
> Gentleness.
> Self-control.

One can easily understand the difference that practicing these "Spirit fruits" would make in any marriage. Can you imagine what a tremendous drop in the present divorce rate there would be if people would live with the aspiration to have the beauty of God in their lives? In many ways, a Christian couple who seeks to honor God in their home is really the Lord's masterpiece, in which He delights to display His greatest skill.

> **I always entertain great hopes.**
>
> **—Robert Frost**

As we look at these characteristics, we begin to understand how a Christian stands out and reflects the glory of God.

Love is giving consideration to the needs of others.

Joy is the product of one's relationship to God. This is where it begins.

Peace with God, with our family, and with others will result in peace within the heart.

Patience is the longsuffering we need as we work with imperfect people such as ourselves.

Kindness is doing good when we see a need.

Goodness is a form of grace, which is manifested by our actions.

Faithfulness is another form of steadfastness and being dependable.

Gentleness leads to a fine spirit that displays real faith.

Self-control is what it all comes down to.

Life takes on significance when people see Christ in us.

6. Permanence—Verse 17B

Here Moses looks upon something that is permanent. As a matter of fact, it is so important that Moses repeats it twice. And what is it?

> Establish thou the work of our hands upon us; yea the work of our hands establish thou it.

Moses is saying in essence,

> Lord, life is so short. Yes, here I am near the century mark, while my brothers and sisters have all died earlier. I would like to do something that will outlast time itself.

And so to many married couples I have said many times, remember your local church is of God and nothing can be more profitable to the kingdom than local churches seeking to carry out God's will. It is a blessing to a church when a husband and wife become actively involved in various ministries of the church. I am thinking of Bob and Julie Huntington and the various jobs they seek to carry out. They prepare communion for 2,500 people once a month. They both usher in the Sunday services. Bob is very much involved in the annual Christmas drama. Julie carries out a weekly Bible study for ladies. Together they have organized a couples' fellowship. They are a blessing to the church because of the example they have set of serving together.

> **Character consists of what you do on the third and fourth tries.**
>
> **—James Michener**

So in verse 17B Moses is saying:

> Lord, my days are numbered; but when I am dead and gone, I want more than a small mound to indicate where I am buried. Rather, I want to give my limited time to a work that will go on and on.

# Wrap Up

What better work is there to do than to encourage and strengthen your local church in its efforts to bring the Word of God to your community and to the world? And where does this goal of significance begin? Right in your home! And when does this begin? Right now, as you set other things aside and seek the face of God in prayer and see what He has in mind for you.

Martin Buber put it this way in his book *Time:*

> Man's earthly task is to realize his created uniqueness. As a Hasidic rabbi called Zusya put it on his deathbed: In the world to come they will not ask me, "Why were you not Moses?" They will ask me, "Why were you not Zusya?"

Yes, we can make a difference, and we start that today.

> **Besides the noble art of getting things done, there is the noble art of leaving things undone. The wisdom of life consists in the elimination of nonessentials.**
> **—Lin Yutang**

# Think About This!

There is a six-fold prescription of how to make life significant. Which ones do you need to consider and when will you start?

# CHAPTER TEN

# Divorce and Remarriage

An important issue facing the church today revolves around this question: Has God made provision for remarriage after divorce? The divorce rate is a huge problem in our society . . . and now in the church as well. In fact, divorce and remarriage are socially acceptable in our society today. Think of the many people you have met in your community, in your workplace, and in your church, who have been divorced and now are remarried.

Why? It brings disorder into the family involved, as well as into society. If there are children, they may well be traumatized by the separation of their parents. In fact, they often are forced to take sides. Divorce also touches the lives of the couples' in-laws, as well as their friends.

In the church, divorce has become a complex problem. In most churches, you have some formerly married couples. You could have a divorced man in the choir, whose ex-wife is sitting in the congregation. She has since remarried. In addition, you could have a woman serving her ex-husband during the communion service.

The sad reality is that some ordained ministers and priests are becoming involved with women sexually. There are even some conservative evangelical ministers whose marriages are breaking up. We have read with alarm the names of several prominent Christian leaders, who have broken their marital vows and now are involved in divorce proceedings.

I was shocked when a Christian colleague of mine divorced his wife because she had put on weight. He said he had lost interest in her and had no desire to have any intimate relationship with her. It would appear that he had forgotten the vow he had made to her: *For better, for worse.* It did not occur to him that he was very much responsible for her welfare. He could have taken steps to understand her condition and discuss what they could do, together, to solve the problem.

In another case, a deacon, in fact the chairman of the board of deacons, divorced his wife just because he got tired of her obnoxious laughter and outspokenness! With such examples by our leaders, is it any wonder that more and more church members are forsaking their own wedding vows?

**Don't speak negatively about your spouse in public or in private.**

When Roman Catholic priests get involved with women, they lose their ministry. In the case of ministers, many move to a church that does not make an issue of it. Some former clergymen, when they separate, will open a counseling office! I was seeking to encourage one pastor, who had left his wife, to get financially resettled. He decided, with his practical experience, to open a counseling clinic. However, he found it was a real problem attracting clients. He did not realize that it would take from five to seven years to build up a business that would support him and, at the same time, provide sufficient support for his family.

**Learn to accept your own mistakes and openly acknowledge them.**

There is much confusion on the teaching of Jesus relative to this important issue of divorce and remarriage. He is very clear about the terms for divorce and remarriage.

The difficulty is found in accepting the Word.

Let's read what Jesus said in His Word, as recorded in Matthew 5:31 and 32.

> It hath been said, Whosoever shall put away his wife, let him give her a writing of divorcement: But I say unto you, That whosoever shall put away his wife, except for the cause of fornication, causeth her to commit adultery: and whosoever shall marry her that is divorced committeth adultery.

What is meant by "fornication"? The Greek word is *porneia*. W.E. Vine states that *porneia* is used to refer to illicit sexual intercourse.

The other main recorded teaching of Jesus on this topic is Mark 10:6-9. Here Jesus is responding to the Pharisees, who were testing Him with a question about putting away one's wife. You will note the clear answer Jesus gives.

> But from the beginning of the creation God made them male and female. For this cause shall a man leave his father and mother, and cleave to his wife; and they twain shall be one flesh: so then they are no more twain, but one flesh. What therefore God hath joined together, let not man put asunder.

Well, the Pharisees were not satisfied with the response, so they went on to ask why Moses allowed divorce. And this is what Jesus says (Mark 10:5, 6, 11, 12):

> And Jesus answered and said unto them, For the hardness of your heart he wrote you this precept. But from the beginning of the creation God made them male and female. . . . And he saith unto them, Whosoever shall put away his wife, and marry another,

**committeth adultery against her. And if a woman shall put away her husband, and be married to another, she committeth adultery.**

In these verses, Jesus also is stating the truth that when a man and a woman marry, they become one flesh. This is what God means when He says in Genesis 2:24:

**Therefore shall a man leave his father and his mother, and shall cleave unto his wife: and they shall be one flesh.**

That word "cleave" is interesting. It represents a very strong bond between the husband and wife. It actually carries the thought of being glued together. In premarital sessions, I give couples two cardboard sheets glued together. The challenge is for them to separate the sheets without ripping them apart. It is impossible. And so it is with marriage. Divorce leaves an indelible mark that cannot be removed by time or circumstances.

**Look at challenges in your own life as an opportunity to grow.**

You know of people whose lives have been shattered by divorce. There is the emotional price to pay. If there are children involved, they are included in the emotional cost. There is a financial price to cover. In my experience of working with divorced people, some have had to pay well over one hundred thousand dollars in separation costs. Of course, there is the dividing up of accumulated stuff. Here again, unless there is mutual agreement between the separating spouses, heated arguments can result over things, many of which have little financial impact but huge emotional significance. The only goal is to gain the upper hand.

**Listen well before you respond to your spouse.**

Another major issue is the sale of the matrimonial home. Children usually will stay put with the custodial parent.

One also must consider other family members, such as in-laws and siblings. Most of the time, friends are brought into the situation and are forced to take sides!

Finally, one of the most serious financial problems results from including a pension in the settlement. This is where one party must come up with a sum that has taken into consideration the future value of their pension.

Now, from Matthew 9, we note that divorce and remarriage are allowed providing we take into consideration the conditional clause, *except for the cause of fornication*. Of course, only the innocent party is allowed to remarry.

The question has been raised, if there has been unfaithfulness, must the couple separate?

The answer is a resounding NO. Is the issue now settled? Not necessarily. This is now a personal matter.

**It's better to solve a problem than win a war.**

Many conservative pastors will not officiate at a remarriage unless they are fairly certain that the former marriage was dissolved due to adultery. Furthermore, a few pastors take the position of not officiating at a remarriage, as they do not want to be in the position of determining if the individuals have the right to remarry.

In l Corinthians 7:15 Paul writes:

> **But if the unbelieving depart, let him depart. A brother or sister is not under bondage in such cases: but God hath called us to peace.**

This verse has led to a variety of excuses for remarriage. I counseled a Christian man, whose wife wished to have her own bedroom as she no longer wished to be intimate with him. His response was to come to me looking for justification for divorce proceedings.

A married couple needs to acknowledge the two main aspects of their marriage. It is both a contract and a covenant. The contract is a legal document between the couple and the state. As such, to break it requires another legal document, such as a divorce or an annulment. However, a covenant is made between the couple and God!

### Change yourself and not your spouse.

A Christian man was divorced but continued to have occasional dates with his ex-wife. This went on for several months. It was not long before they developed a strong bond, which eventually led to a discussion of remarriage. This continued for several weeks until they agreed that their divorce, on the grounds of incompatibility, was a serious error.

They set a wedding date and decided to purchase a new house and start over. Assurance was given that though they were divorced as far as the state was concerned, according to the Scriptures, they were still married. With this, we planned a marriage service to meet the civic needs, but that in reality it was a reaffirmation of their earlier wedding vows.

The fact that our secular society has introduced no-fault divorce makes it easy to break up a marriage. In a sense, marriage today is a tentative situation. Anyone can dissolve a marriage and remarry. And many times, a husband or wife will announce their engagement before the ink has dried on their divorce document. Let a husband or wife claim incompatibility or irreconcilable differences, and a divorce can be granted, whether the other party agrees or not. In a sense, divorce is almost non-adversarial from the court's perspective.

In my premarital sessions, I emphasize ongoing courting. It's important for a husband to realize that when he marries a wife, courtship must not stop at the wedding altar. It is an ongoing process.

**Say something nice to your spouse on a daily basis.**

Have you heard of what I call *Marriage Dividends?* Consider your marriage as a bank account, where you make deposits such as a positive word of encouragement or a deed that shows your love and respect. For instance:

> **That was a nice meal.**
> **Thanks for picking up those items for me.**
> **I like the way you look today.**
> **It was thoughtful of you to call me at the office.**

You can think of hundreds of ways to deposit dividends in your marriage. Of course, it is important that you mean what you say. Do this on a daily basis, and you soon build up a fine marriage bank. This, of course, is what marriage is all about: husband and wife blessing each other. Furthermore, if you have children, you are setting a splendid example of how to establish positive interpersonal relationships.

The final word is from our Lord, who taught that divorce is not in the will of God. God made us, male and female, one man for one woman. It is not the will of God for either husband or wife to have multiple spouses. It is clearly stated in Genesis 2:24 that in marriage two become one. One to marry another. There is no place or room for a third one!

I like the way my pastor, Charles Price, of The Peoples Church, Toronto, Canada, summarizes the divorce issue:

> **There are many pastoral concerns that come out of this, of course, and it is a complex issue in many ways, but our pastoral care must derive from our theological understanding of scripture. Hence our "view" must be the expression of Scripture, and, in particular, it must harmonize with the teaching of Jesus. If it does not, we have ceased to act Christianly.**

There are those who say that we are becoming legalists because we accept and apply the teaching of Jesus on divorce. This is not so! Rather, it is a confirmation of our respect for the Word of God and our desire to carry out the command of Jesus.

> **For this is the love of God, that we keep his commandments (1 John 5:3).**

In the beginning, God instituted marriage so that men and women would have a lifelong commitment that is not to be severed.

Marriages that seek to honor Jesus Christ and are built on love, kindness, and respect for each other will last a lifetime! In addition, marriage provides a home where children have the benefit of both a father and a mother. The marriage breakups that are rampant today are not part of God's original plan. Instead, they show how many have rejected God's will regarding marriage.

# Bibliography for Second Marriages

Ahrons, Constance and Roy Rogers. *Divorced From Divorce.* New York City, NY: A Wiley Imprint, 2003.

Allen. Marvin. *Angry Men, Passive Men.* New York: Fawcett Columbine, 1993.

Barbach, Lonnie and David Geisinger. *Going the Distance.* Toronto: Doubleday, 1991.

Bell, Melvin. *Divorcing.* New York: St. Martin's Press, 1988.

Bergen, Marja. *Riding the Roller Coaster.* Kelowna, BC: Northstone, 1999.

Betcher, William. *Intimate Play.* New York: Viking Press, 1987.

Bloch, Jon. *The Everything Health Guide.* Avon, MA: Adams Media, 2006.

*The Book of Common Prayer.* Toronto: The Anglican Church, 1962.

Bray, James and John Kelly. *Step Families.* New York: Broadway, 1998.

Broersma, Margaret. *Daily Reflections for Stepparents.* Grand Rapids, MI: Kregel, 2003.

Broersma, Margaret. *Stepparent to Stepparent.* Grand Rapids, MI: Kregel, 2004.

Caine, Lynn. *Being A Widow.* New York: Arbor House, 1988.

Campbell, Scott and Phyllis Silverman. *Widower.* New York: Prentice Hall Press, 1987.

Castle, Lana. *Bipolar Disorder Demystified.* New York: Marlowe, 2003.

Chapman, Gary. *Desperate Marriages.* New York: Moody Press, 1999.

Coates, Christine and Robert Rogers. *Divorced Families.* New York: W.W. Norton and Company, 1989.

Coates, Christine and Robert LaCrosse. *Learning From Divorce.* A Wiley Imprint, 2003.

Cochrane, Michael. *Surviving Your Divorce.* Toronto: John Wiley, 2007.

Donaldson, Corey. *Don't You Dare Get Married Until You Read This.* New York: Three Rivers Press, 2001.

Edelman, Alice and Roy Stuzin. *How To Survive A Second Marriage.* Atascadero, CA: Lyle Stuart Publishers, 1980.

Efron, Ronald. *Letting Go of Anger.* Oakland, CA: New Harabinger Publications, 2006.

Eggerichs, Emerson. *Cracking the Communication Code.* Colorado Springs, CO: Focus on the Family, 2007.

Egner, David. *What Is the Promise of Marriage?* Grand Rapids, MI: Radio Bible Class, 2007.

Eisendrath, Polly. *You're Not What I Expected.* New York: William Morrow and

Company, 1993.

Engel, Beverly. *Loving Him Without Losing Him.* New York: John Wiley and

Sons, 2000.

Exley, Richard. *Living in Harmony.* Forest Green, AR: New Leaf Press, 2003.

Fein, Ellen and Sherrie Schneider. *The Rules for Marriage.* New York: Warner Books, 2001.

Fields, Susan. *Getting Married Again.* New York: Dodd Mead, 1975.

Fisher, Gary. *Rebuilding When Your Relationship Ends.* Atascadero, CA: Impact, 2004.

Frisbie, David and Lisa Frisbie. *Happily Remarried.* Eugene, OR: Harvest House, 2005.

Fram, Leslie. *How to Marry a Divorced Man.* New York: Regal, 2004.

Gates, Philomene. *Suddenly Alone.* Toronto: Harper and Row, 1990.

Grant, Audrey. *Ex Etiquette: The Etiquette of Separation, Divorce & Remarriage.* Toronto: Prentice House, 1998.

Gray, John. *Men, Women and Relationships.* New York: Quill, 2002.

Greenwald, Rachel. *Find a Husband After 35.* New York: Ballabtine, 2003.

Grenier, Guy. *The Ten Conversations.* New York: Key Porter, 2007.

Grissom, Steve and Kathy Leonard. *Divorce Care,* Nashville, TN: Nelson Books, 2005.

Harley, Willard. *I Promise You.* Grand Rapids, MI: Revell, 1998.

Harper, Lisa. *Holding Out for a Hero.* Wheaton, IL: Tyndale, 2005.

Heald, Jack and Cynthia Heald. *Walking Together.* Colorado Springs, CO: NavPress, 2000.

Heim, Toben and Joanne Heim. *Happily Ever After.* Grand Rapids, MI: Kregel, 2006.

Herrick, Charles. *100 Questions & Answers About Alcoholism.* Boston; Jones and Bartlett, 2007.

Janda, Louis and Ellen MacCormack. *The Second Time Around.* Secaucus, NJ: Carol Publishing, 1991.

Kamm, Phyllis. *Remarriage.* Hayward, CA: Bristol Publishing, 1991.

Kelly, Susan and Dale Burg. *The Second Time Around.* New York: Harper, 2000.

Kirshenbau, Mira. *Our Love Is Too Good to Feel So Bad.* New York: Avon Books, 1998.

Kottler, Jeffrey. *Beyond Blame.* San Francisco, CA: Jossey Books, 1994.

Krantzler, Mel and Patricia Krantzler. *The New Creative Divorce.* Avon, MA: Adams Media Corporation, 1998.

Kniskern, Joseph. *When the Vow Breaks.* Nashville, TN: Broadman and Holman Publishers, 1998.

Littauer, Marita. *Love Extravagantly.* Minneapolis, MN: Bethany, 2001.

Littauer, Marita and Chuck Noon. *Tailor Made Marriage.* Grand Rapids, MI: Kregel, 2006.

MacDonald, Gordon. *Ordering Your Private World*. Nashville, TN: Thomas Nelson, 1985.

Manzardo, Ann and others. *Alcoholism*. New York: Oxford Press, 2006.

Meberg, Marilyn. *Since You Asked*. Nashville, TN: Nelson, 2006.

Moschetta, Evelyn and Paul Moschetta. *The Marriage Spirit*. New York: Simon and Schuster, 1998.

McGraw, Robin. *From My Heart to Yours*. Nashville, TN: Nelson, 2007.

McKay, Matthew. *When Anger Hurts*. Oakland, CA: New Harbinger Publications, 1989.

McManamy, John. *Living Well With Depression and Bipolar Disorder*. New York: Collins, 2006.

Naylor, Sharon. *1,000 Ways to Have a Dazzling Second Wedding*. Franklin Lake, NJ: New Page Books, 2001.

Osborne, Cecil. *The Art of Understanding Yourself*. Grand Rapids, MI: Zondervan, 1976.

Outcalt, Todd. *Before You Say I Do*. New York: The Berkley Publishing Group, 1998.

Parrott, Les and Leslie Parrott. *The Love List*. Grand Rapids, MI; Zondervan, 2002.

Parrott, Les and Leslie Parrott. *Saving Your Second Marriage Before It Starts*. Grand Rapids, MI: Zondervan, 2001.

Powell, John. *The Secret of Staying in Love*. Niles, IL: Argus Communications, 1974.

Raffel, Lee. *Should I Stay or Go?* Chicago: Contemporary Books, 1997.

Redding, Mary Lou. *Breaking and Mending*. Nashville, TN: Upper Room, 2000.

Rogers, Victoria. *Finding a Man Worth Keeping*. West Monroe, LA: Howard Publishing, 2005.

Rusren, Sharon and Michael Rusren. *The One Year Book on Church History*. Nashville, TN: Tyndale Press, 2003.

Smalley, Gary. *Secrets to Lasting Love*. New York: Simon and Schuster, 2000.

Smith, Debra. *Marriage Revolution*. Eugene, OR: Harvest, 2007.

Smith, Harold. *Grievers Ask.* Minneapolis, MN: Augsburg Books, 2004.

Smith, Lori. *The Single Truth.* Shippensburg, PA: Destiny Image, 2002.

Stedman, Rick. *Your Single Treasure.* Nashville, TN: Nelson Publishers, 1993.

Stoop, David and Jan Stoop. *The Intimacy Factor.* Nashville, TN: Nelson Publishers, 1993.

Tauber, Edward and Jim Smoke. *Finding the Right One After Divorce.* Eugene, OR: Harvest, 2007.

Thomas, Angela. *My Single Mom.* Nashville, TN: Nelson, 2007.

Trafford, Abigail. *Crazy Time.* New York: Harper, 1982.

Vine, W.E. *Expository Dictionary of New Testament Words.* Westwood, NJ: Revell, 1962.

Wallerstein, Judith and Sandra Blakeslee. *The Good Marriages.* Boston: Houghton Mifflin Company, 1995.

Westheimer, Ruth. *Rekindling Romance for Dummies.* Foster City, CA: IDG Books Worldwide, Inc, 2001.

Whelchel, Mary. *Common Mistakes Singles Make.* Toronto: Revell, 1999.

Wilson, Meg. *Hope After Betrayal.* Grand Rapids, MI: Kregel, 2007.

Wright, II, Norman. *Before You Remarry.* Eugene, OR: Harvey Press, 1999.

Wright, H. Norman. *Relationships That Work.* Ventura, CA: Regal, 1998.

Wyeth, Sharon. *Ginger Brown: Too Many Houses.* New York: Random House, 1996.